THE JOURNEY CONTINUES VOL.9

SEARCHING FOR DESTINY AND PURPOSE

WILLIAM HATFIELD

WILLIAM HATFIELD

Copyright © 2019 WILLIAM HATFIELD

All rights reserved.

ISBN:
978-1-7750330-9-7

DEDICATION

I DEDICATE THIS BOOK TO THE THIRSTY AND HUNGRY SAINTS OF GOD THAT DESIRE AN INTIMACY WITH THE HOLY SPIRIT LIKE NO OTHER. MY PRAYER IS THAT YOU CAN FIND THIS JOURNEY AS A SOURCE OF ENCOURAGEMENT, STRENGTH AND POWER TO OVERCOME LIFE'S STRUGGLES AND WALK IN A GREATER SENSE OF FREEDOM AND RELATIONSHIP WITH THE HOLY SPIRIT AND ALL WITHIN YOUR SPHERE OF INFLUENCE.

PROLOGUE

Everyone is on a journey to answer some important questions in life. Who am I? Why was I born? What's my purpose? DOES I Just exist or do I have a destiny that is greater than my imagination? In this book I am on a search for my destiny and place in the universal body of Christ. I am revisiting events, dreams and visions that may have left clues as to my purpose and destiny in Christ

ACKNOWLEDGMENTS

We are all on a journey through life! I want to thank all my family and friends who stand besides me and encourage me when times are tough.

I especially want to thank my aunt Viola for all her work in editing and preparing the first manuscript for publishing. The knowledge I gained helped me to discover a journey into writing

CONTENTS

DEDICATION   i
PROLOGUE
Acknowledgments

1	REVELATION	Pg. 2
2	HINDERANCES TO THE SUPERNATURAL	Pg. 15
3	CARES OF LIFE	Pg. 21
4	TRADITIONS OF MEN	Pg. 26
5	LACK OF KNOWLEDGE	Pg. 31
6	DECEPTION-SUBSTITUTION	Pg. 38
7	INTIMIDATION	Pg. 65
8	REVEALING OF SIN	Pg. 72
9	WORDS	Pg. 89
10	POWERFUL INSTRUMENTS	Pg. 102

CONTENTS CONTINUED

11 THE SUPERNATURAL FLOOD OF GOD..................PG. 107
12 JOURNEY TO THE GLORY.................................PG. 132
   13 ENCOURAGEMENT...PG. 144
    14 PSALMIST..PG 155
     15 THE CALL..pg.219
     16 CONFIRMATION OF THE CALL........................pg.228
     17 THE ANOINTING...pg. 261
     18 EVIDENCE OF THE ANOINTING......................pg.266
     19 DREAMS..pg. 275
    20 VISIONS..PG.302
    21 THE HEART..PG.318
    22 OPINIONS..PG.325
   23 CHARACTER..PG.329
   24 THE MIND..PG.332
   25 MY WILL_MOTIVES...PG.335
   26 OPENING THE BOOK OF YOUR HEART.............PG.340

   27 WORDS AND DESTINY.......................................PG.346

   28 DESIRE..PG.358

   29 DESTINY AND PURPOSE....................................PG.364

   ABOUT THE AUTHOR..PG.365

1 REVELATION

The words REPENTANCE BEFORE RESURRECTION struck my spirit like a bolt of lightning. The anointing of the Holy Spirit began to flow right there in that moment. I put down the book I was reading on prayer and allowed the Holy Spirit to take me wherever He wanted me to go.

In my spirit, pictures and sounds became alive as I was brought back to the days of my conversion to Christ. I had received Christ into my heart as a young boy while attending a Pentecostal Bible camp. My cousin had an Aunt Ethel and Uncle Henry; they had asked my parents for permission for my sister and me to attend the meetings with them.

I was approximately ten years old when I attended that bible camp. I am sure that

Aunt Ethel and Uncle Henry never realized the impact that God was about to have on that young boy.

Bible camp was filled with activities to keep young boys excited and interested. One evening after the Bible message, an alter call was given and I found myself at the alter giving my heart to Jesus. With tears streaming down my face, I asked Jesus to come into my heart.

As a young child I never really understood a lot of what I was taught about Jesus. One thing that I knew for sure was that Jesus loved us and would never hurt us. At- tending the country Baptist church was the highlight of my week. I really enjoyed church, hearing the stories, making crafts, and meeting new people. This particular day seemed like any other day in a long endless succession of days that was filled with chores and playtime. That evening was like any other evening, supper time, homework, a little television and then off to bed.

As I put my head on the pillow I remembered to pray. During church I remember hearing about a devil that liked to hurt people but, also heard how to make him go away as well. I couldn't quite remember the word my cousin told me to use so I would say, "devil I refugee you in the Name of Jesus, you stay away from my family." It wasn't until a few years later that I realized the word was rebuke rather than refugee; but to a little child it did not matter what the word was as long as the devil stayed away.

Unknown to me the Holy Spirit was planning a supernatural visitation as soon as the household had retired for the night. Upon entering into the early hours of the morning; a light illuminating the interior of our house awakened me. Something was drawing me to the source of the light. As I walked into the kitchen I realized the light stated outside radiating in. I was compelled to go outside to the steps. The most marvelous sight I had ever seen appeared in the sky above me. A large pair of hands appeared in the sky held together in prayer. The hands began to open and a bible appeared. This bible was so huge it seemed to fill the entire sky. I stood in awe as a passage of scripture was circled.

The scripture was Ezekiel 3:10-11, "Moreover He said to me: "Son of man, receive into your heart all my words that I speak to you, and hear with your ears. And go, get to the captives, to the children of your people, and speak to them and tell them, 'Thus says the Lord God,' whether they hear, or whether they refuse."

After a minute or so of watching this scene I was translated to the far end of our grain field. My brothers and sisters were with me. We were standing beside the flat top hay wagon when Jesus appeared. He was wearing royal purple robes and radiated the most brilliant light I had ever seen. The glory radiating from Christ was so brilliant that creation ceased to exist, all you could see was Jesus and His glory, and nothing else was visible.

Jesus stood before us, His hand extended to us. In His hand was a piece of fruit of some sort. He presented this fruit to us, we all stood staring not sure what to do. I took the fruit from His hand and stood in amazement looking at this fruit, as it was not like anything we had ever seen. I decided to take a bite of the fruit. As soon as I bit off a piece of the fruit, the vision ended, I was sitting on the edge of my bed, daylight pouring in through the windows, leaving me wondering about the events that just took place.

    I never really understood that vision as a child, but one thing was very clear to me; from that time on I wanted to be a minister of the Gospel of Jesus Christ.

I tried to share that Vision and my desire to be a minister of the gospel, with family but my family never seemed to understand what was going on in my life. My mother just watched me grow in my desire for God. Several years later on her deathbed, she told me of a time when she found me running around in the house with a bible in my hand. She asked me what I was doing and I told her I was chasing after God. She then told me I couldn't catch God and that I was to sit still and let Him catch me.

One church meeting stands out strong in my mind since it was probably one of the last meetings I attended as a child. A young girl sang a special song in which I found great pleasure. I started clapping wanting to show appreciation for the beautiful song she sung. The Pastor chewed me out severely in front of the congregation; he then proceeded to smack my hands with a pointer stick for not having respect for the things of God. I never could figure out how clapping showed disrespect for God. This form of rejection convinced me to stay away from church and anything to do with God.

When the church rejects its own you can be sure the devil will be right there to welcome them. The only thing the devil doesn't tell those who are being rejected by the church are; that he is out to abuse them and eventually destroy them. I found this out first hand, as I became drawn into the occult through the medium of comic books and rock music.

At the age of fifteen I left home to discover what life was all about. I entered the world of alcohol, drugs, sleazy women and occult activity. The memory of my Visitation from Jesus was driven far from my mind. I pursued this lifestyle with all my strength, believing this to be the life of excitement and intrigue I was searching for.

In October of 1981, I married a young woman who also had some experience in the occult; however this lifestyle was not at all what I thought it to be. I decided to settle down and search for a lifestyle that would be fulfilling. Out of nowhere people stared to come across my path and tell me about Jesus and His love. I was not ready to hear their message, because I associated Christianity with the rejection I experienced as a child. Nevertheless the Word of God was sown in my heart.

    The spring of 1982 was a turning Point in my life, which would also affect the lives of others around me. Little did I realize that though I walked away from Jesus; HE never walked away from me?
In April of 1982 Jesus visited me for the second time. This Visitation caused me to return to the Lord Jesus Christ with a fervent zealousness that still continues in my heart today.
The visitation started with the following scenes taking place: My fellow workers from the muffler shop and I were partying at a South American colonial style mansion. There was an abundance of drinking and carousing. I was participating fully when all of a sudden something started to bother my spirit. I did not understand what was

happening, but I knew I had to ask God to forgive me for the lifestyle I had indulged in. Seeking privacy, I exited to a balcony overlooking a garden. I started to repent and tell God that I was sorry when I heard a voice say, "Forget it" I was startled and looked around to see who was playing a joke on me. Not finding anyone I continued to ask God's forgiveness. Again I heard a voice say, "Forget it." I looked around a second time, finding no one. This time I was compelled to look into the sky. As I watched the sky, an amazing thing happened.

    A strange but beautiful presence surrounded me as I watched the clouds change shapes. The clouds changed into a variety of different animals. A voice filled with love and peace spoke from among the animal shaped clouds. In my heart I knew I was talking with God. The voice proceeded to say, "Forget it, I want you to listen to my son Jesus, and if you can't make it, grab onto one of the animals and it will bring you to heaven where you belong. I reached up and grabbed the leg of the closest animal, which happened to be a lamb. Suddenly, I found myself running along a vast expanse of beach. Beautiful, peaceful, and exhilarating was this place I was in. I looked out over a huge ocean and was aware that everything I could see was created just for me. I was totally amazed at my surroundings, especially the peace I experienced.

Suddenly I was removed from that place and a new scene unfolded before my eyes. I could see a Jesus, standing beside a large rock, watching over his sheep. I watched this scene with interest for few minutes. This scene disappeared and I was back at the balcony looking into the sky.

Again the voice of the Lord spoke to me saying, "Forget it, all I want you to do is listen to my Son." At this point I made an unbelieving arrogant statement toward God. Why you might ask would a person make arrogant statements toward God. It is quite simple; being influenced in the occult and street gangs you are taught how to rebel against all authority. To my surprise He responded with authority and sternness, I sensed that if I didn't stop being ignorant my life could be easily finished at that point. Even though God responded with sternness the great love He has for His creation never left His voice. Adamantly the Lord said, "LISTEN TO MY SON JESUS." After this statement the visitation ended.

1. Jesus was not telling me to forget about repentance. He was referring to my former lifestyle along with the guilt and fear. By saying forget it He was telling me that He wasn't holding my past against me. The Lord was also implying that I should forget about my past and follow Jesus.

PHILIPPIANS 3:13-14, "Brethren, I do not count myself to have apprehended; but one thing I do, forgetting those things which are behind and reaching forward to those things which are ahead, I press toward the goal for the Prize of the upward call of God in Christ Jesus."

I awoke from my sleep the following morning totally turned on for Jesus Christ. I consumed the Word of God for the next year. Everywhere I went I was aware of the presence of the Lord with me. Little over a year later my wife Carrie came to the Lord through visitation of her own. Thus began the most exciting life I ever experienced. Receiving the baptism of the Holy Ghost with the evidence of speaking in tongues made our lives even more exciting. This was the lifestyle we were searching for.

Soon the Gifts of the Holy Ghost began to manifest in our lives, which only increases our zeal. The Lord began to speak with us through visions and dreams on a regular basis. Jesus appeared to my wife and I many times encouraging, loving and strengthening us in our walk with Him. In the following chapters I would like to share a few of the visions and dreams Jesus gave us.

    I pray that the Holy Spirit will cause you to walk closer to Jesus after reading these writings. I know my walk has become stronger for Christ and my zeal has increased after the Holy Spirit revealed the following visions and dreams to me.

2 HINDRANCES TO THE SUPERNATURAL

We (my family) were spending the night at my cousin's place one night while he was out of town. My wife Carrie and I spent the evening discussing the Word of God and encouraging my cousin's wife. At eleven o'clock I retired for the night. As I went to sleep the Holy Spirit began to invade my dreams.

This dream began with me lying on a bed asleep. I was suddenly, awakened becoming aware of a great amount of activity outside. I looked out the bedroom window to find daylight streaming in at me. I noticed people were lifting off the ground as if some unseen force were picking them up. These people rose higher and higher. As soon they were as high as the clouds, they disappeared from my sight. The thought that struck me was that this is the resurrection of the church the bible talks about.

Suddenly I sensed the Spirit of God move over me and gently pick me off the floor. What a magnificent feeling as waves of pleasure swept through my entire being, but, soon the euphoria turn to dread. I could not get any higher than the ceiling. After a couple of attempts to go higher the Holy Spirit dropped me back to the bed and quickly moved out of the house.

    I awoke the next morning, very concerned, thinking I had missed the resurrection of the church. This dream really bothered me so I began to make phone calls to people I knew would go to heaven when the resurrection happened. Imagine my anxiety when nobody answered the phone after the first few calls. Finally to my relief the phone was answered. I shared my dream with that individual and expressed my relief of not missing resurrection day.

    I became puzzled as to the meaning of this dream. It wasn't many years later that I received the interpretation of the dream. November 1989, while sitting quietly, reading a book on prayer, the Holy Spirit spoke "REPENTANCE BEFORE RESURRECTION" to my spirit. Those words exploded in my heart and brought forth the revelation of the aforementioned dream.

This dream was dealing with people on a personal, individual level. God's resurrection power is trying to come on individuals to raise them up to experience the supernatural manifestations of the Holy Spirit. These supernatural experiences will peak with the resurrection of the Church. God's will for His people is that they walk in the supernatural. God wants every member of the Body of Christ to walk as Jesus walked. Jesus healed the sick, cleansed lepers and spoke the Word of God with authority and wisdom that stunned the people of that time. God would he pleased if we operated like Jesus, healing the sick and speaking His Word with such authority so as to confound the people of our time as well.

In this dream the people who were raised from the ground represented those who allow the Holy Spirit to have His way in their lives. By raising these people higher than the clouds and eventually out of sight, a relationship between the natural and supernatural is drawn. The natural man has little or no understanding of the spirit man. The spirit man will walk in areas, and understand the ways of God, that the natural man cannot perceive or see.

The spirit man will walk in the abundant life mentioned by Jesus. In John 14:12 Jesus said we would do greater works. The spirit man will fulfill Jesus' words by accomplishing the greater works. Jesus will also receive worship through their exploits. The natural man would only look on in amazement as the spirit man ascends to greater plateaus.

While many individuals will experience the supernatural, some will not. The Holy Spirit is trying to bring everyone into a supernatural walk. The part of the dream where the Holy Spirit moved upon me to raise me up represents the Spirit's desire for all to be supernatural. The part of the dream where I could not get through the ceiling represented hindrances in my life that prevented me from going on into the supernatural.

At the time of the resurrection of the Church, a ceiling or any other physical object will have no effect on us, nor will it be a slow ascension as the dream was. I Corinthians 15:52 say the Church will resurrect in a moment, in the twinkling of an eye.

The lesson the Lord was trying to get across is the fact that there are hindrances not only in my life but also in the lives of other Christians. Even though I had experienced the Holy Ghost in my life on a grand scale there are many hindrances that I need to deal with.

Let's look into the scriptures to find these

hindrances that keep us from a greater supernatural walk.

GALATIANS 5:7, "You ran well. Who hindered you from obeying the truth?" The word "hindered" here means to beat back. Hebrews 12:1, "Therefore we also, since we are sur- rounded by so great a cloud of witnesses, let us lay aside every weight and the sin which so easily ensnares us, and let us run with endurance the race that is set before us." The Greek word for weight in this verse is "ogkos" which means a mass, burden or hindrance.

We have two situations to look at; 1) The Christian is carrying a mass or burden, which is hindering the supernatural walk; 2) The Christian is being beaten back by some outside force in an effort to prevent a supernatural walk. Let's take a look at some basic areas that hinder Christians from walking into the supernatural.

3 CHRISTIANS CARRYING BURDENS: THE CARES OF LIFE

Now these are the ones sown among thorns: they are the ones who hear the word, and the cares of this world, the deceitfulness of riches, and the desires for other things entering in choke the word, and becomes unfruitful," Mark 4:18-19. "The ones that fell among thorns are those who, when they have heard the Word, go out and are choked with cares, riches, and pleasures of life, and bring no fruit to maturity," Luke 8:14.

To walk in the supernatural is to walk in the Word of God. When we give the Word of God top priority in our life, the Word will lead you into supernatural manifestations. When we allow the cares of this world, the deceitfulness of riches, and the pleasures of life to have top priority, the Word becomes unfruitful and does not produce results.

Christians all across our nation are so caught up with the pursuit of material things they have no time for prayer, Bible study and the pursuit of spiritual principles. I know Christians who are so caught up with the pleasures of life that the world offers, that they have forgotten about Godly standards. These people have deceived themselves; they are in a vicious circle of destruction.

    Do you realize that the cares of life creates an attitude of selfishness in people? When the Bible talks about the cares of life it is referring to being anxious, worried or distracted about your life to the point of being overwhelmed. When the cares of life enter in, a person becomes consumed about his/her own survival. How am I going to pay the bills? How do I eat? DO I have enough to pay my tithes? How can I help others when I am so helpless in my own eyes? Soon you get to a place where you no longer reach out to others. Doubt and unbelief settle in your heart and you begin to block God's provision for your life. When doubt and unbelief settle in a man's heart he becomes hard hearted and ignores the needs of others. (Hardhearted people will never move into supernatural manifestations of the Word of God.) When you look at Jesus' life and ministry the needs of others were met.

If the cares of life have you trapped, repent, then go find a need in the life of someone and meet it at any cost. If you do that you will bust the back of that problem that keeps you down. When you make it a habit of reaching out to others the cares of life will be powerless in Satan's efforts to keep you in bondage.

    We do not have to be concerned for our own lives because God has given us the greatest provision available, HIS WORD. Continual study and practice of the Word of God will cause you to never be weighed down with the cares of life. We must put our trust and confidence in God's Word.

God teaches us to reach out to others and trust Him to pro- vide for us. Revelation 12:11, "and they did not love their lives to the death." Jesus came and gave Himself for us, so how much more should we give of ourselves, to His Body the Church?

Jesus warns us in His Word about the cares of life. Luke 21:34-36, "But take heed to yourselves, lest your hearts be weighed down with carousing, drunkenness, and the CARES OF this LIFE, and that day come on you unexpectedly.
For it will come as a snare on all those who dwell on the face of the whole earth; Watch therefore, and pray always that you may be counted worthy to escape all these things that will come to pass, and to stand before the son of man."
Let us cast aside the cares of life. Determine in your heart to live a repentant life before God. Look to the Word of God daily for your provision. Reach out to meet the needs of others. Looking to the Word daily will help

you to be free from the cares of life. 1 Peter 5:7 "Casting all your cares upon him, for He cares for you."

HOW GOD USES YOU IS NOT DEPENDENT UPON HOW MUCH YOU HAVE, BUT ON YOUR OBEDIENCE TO THE WORD OF GOD.

4 TRADITIONS OF MEN: MAJOR HINDRANCE TO BELIEVERS

Traditions and philosophies of men will definitely hinder your walk in the supernatural. Did you know that every denomination we have today is the result of men getting
Hold of and controlling a move of God? Denominations were not started by God but by men. A denomination gets started by taking a present day move of the Spirit of God and building an entire church structure on the truth God revealed. When God begins to move in a different direction tradition rears its head in protest. Tradition is simply a nice word for trying to tell God that He cannot do anything, or restore a truth to the Body of Christ, other than that which my particular denomination believes.

One definition of philosophy is a search for a general understanding of values and reality by chiefly SPECULATIVE means. Speculate also means to ASSUME.

People who are philosophical have very few absolutes in their lives. They try to figure God out by using their five senses rather than God's Word. If you give them a choice between God's Word and their five senses, the five senses would prevail. People who are traditionally or denominational oriented will hold fast to their philosophies, or those of their churches, even if it is in complete opposition to the Word of God.

I remember one denominational church I attended; the governing board for all of North America was having a vote on a subject that caused controversy within that group. This group discussed the issue and cast their vote. The end result of their discussion was that the baptism of the Holy Ghost with the evidence of speaking in tongues was definitely of the devil and that their churches and members were not to partake of it.

When the Bible disagrees with denominational doctrine, tradition says to disagree with the Bible. I remember hearing about one church organization stating that if they were to cast off their tradition they would have to dissolve their entire organization.

No wonder Jesus was very upset with the Pharisees when He said in Mark 7:6-7, "well did ISAIAH prophesy to you hypocrites, as it is written: 'this people honor me with their lips, but their heart is far from me. And in vain they worship me, teaching as doctrines the commandments of men."

"And He said to them, all too well you reject the commandment of God, that you may keep your tradition.

 Making the Word of God of 'N0 effect through your tradition which you have handed down," Mark 7:9.13.

"Beware lest anyone cheat you through philosophy and empty deceit, according to the tradition of men, according to the basic principles of the world, and not according to Christ," Colossians 2:8.

You decide what you want to do. Do you want to hold to your traditions and philosophies over the Word of God? Do you want to hold the Word of God above traditions and philosophies? By holding onto things other than Christ, you cheat yourself from the supernatural manifestations of the Word of God. You may even find that tradition can even cheat you out of salvation. Hold onto Christ with all your might for then you will find supernatural life.

"For this commandment which I command you today, it is not too mysterious for you, nor is it far off. It is not in heaven that you should say:' who will ascend into heaven for us and bring it to us; that we may hear it and do it?' Nor is it beyond the sea that you should say 'who will go over the sea and bring it to us that we may hear it and do it?' But the word is very near you, in your mouth and in your heart, that you may do it." See, I have set before you today life and good, death and evil," in that I command you today to love the Lord your God, to walk in His ways, and to keep His commandments, His statutes, and His judgments, that you may live and multiply; and the Lord your God will bless you in the land which you go to possess. But if your heart turns away so that you do not hear, and are drawn away, and worship other gods (traditions) and serve them, I announce to you today that you shall surely perish; you shall not pro- long your days in the land which you cross over the Jordan to go in and possess. "I call heaven and earth as witness to- day against you, that I have set before you life and death, blessings and cursing; therefore choose life, that both you and your descendants may live;" that you CLING TO HIM, FOR HE IS YOUR LIFE AND LENGTH OF YOUR

DAYS; and that you may dwell in the land which the Lord swore to your fathers, to Abraham, Isaac, and Jacob, to give them." Deuteronomy 30:11-20.

5 LACK OF KNOWLEDGE

Lack of knowledge of God's Word is a major hindrance to your walk in the supernatural realm. The evidence is overwhelming when we look at the condition our churches are in. We argue and fight with each other over scriptures and doctrine continually. I imagine we could tolerate differences on doctrines that aren't clearly defined in the Word, but we fight over doctrines, which are plain and obvious. Hebrews 6:12 are a perfect example of doctrines we fight over. "Therefore, leaving the discussion of the elementary principles of Christ, let us go on to perfection, not laying again the foundation of the repentance from dead works and of faith toward God, of the doctrine of baptisms, of laying on of hands, of resurrection of the dead, and of eternal judgment."
The Bible calls these principles elementary, meaning they are our foundation. How can

we move on into the supernatural realm of God when we haven't established our foundation properly?

"My people are destroyed for a lack of knowledge. Because you have rejected knowledge, I will also reject you from being priests for me; because you have forgotten the law of your God, I will also forget your children," Hosea 4:6.

This scripture is being fulfilled right before our very eyes today. Organizations of religious natures have rejected the knowledge of God and are reaping their rewards. God is rejecting them as priests and credible ministers of the gospel. When a church organization rejects the Word of God, evil creeps in under the disguise of "the new morality." When homosexuality becomes an issue (should I allow it in my church or should I disallow it) in any church organization, it is time to pray that God would lead you to a Bible believing God-fearing church. To have a homosexual try and teach me about a God who smiles on his immoral activities especially when the Bible condemns such activities sits in the same category as a Satanist trying to teach me about the love of Satan.

When the knowledge of God is rejected, all kinds of evil doctrine will take place in the hearts of men. When you do not see the Holy Spirit moving in your church, you had better check the doctrine being preached.

"And they went out and preached everywhere, the Lord working with them and confirming the word through accompanying signs. Amen." Mark 16:20. Mark 16:17-18 tells us the signs that accompany the true Word of God being preached, "And these signs will follow those who believe: In my name they will cast out demons; they will speak with new tongues; they will take up serpents; and if they drink anything deadly, it will by no means hurt them; they will lay hands on the sick, and they will recover."

DON'T BE FOUND BY GOD REJECTING

ANY PORTION OF THE KNOWLEDGE OF GOD.

Each individual must stand before God alone and answer for his own life. You cannot blame a church, ministry, organization, or a preacher for the short falls in your life. You will stand or fall before God based on your own merits. If a church or ministry is preaching doctrines other than what the Word teaches, you will have to decide if you will stay there or move on. I would encourage you to seek after the knowledge of God. Find churches and ministries that will help you in your search. The Bible says that God will reward those that diligently seek after Him. When you seek after the Word of God with all your heart, get prepared to experience a supernatural life. The supernatural life is the most exciting, vibrant, joyful life you can experience.

2) Galatians 5:7, who hindered (beat back, prevented) you from obeying the truth?

In the first section we looked at a Christian's number one enemy, himself/herself who prevents the supernatural lifestyle from happening in their lives. Once we have committed ourselves to go on with God, repented of sin, studying the Word and reaching out to others, we run into our number two enemy, the devil.

The reason I call him our number two enemy is because he is not as powerful as our number one enemy, which is ourselves. Satan cannot make you do anything you do not want to do. He has the power to influence but does not have the power to control a born again Christian. Satan fears Christians who decide to become supernatural simply because he loses his power to influence them. The supernatural Christian soon learns the weapons of his warfare and continually defeats Satan at every turn. The supernatural Christian learns to deal with the spiritual manipulation that causes people to do hurtful things to other people. Fighting the devil that is working behind the scenes is more productive than fighting with people. Satan tries to hide the supernatural life God wants to bless us with because he knows it will mean his downfall if we ever clue in to God's victorious lifestyle for us. Listen, if you have a problem believing the supernatural is for Christians, merely take a look at what Satan tries to imitate. He tries to show the world that the church is a boring, nothing happening organization that puts people into bondage through rules and regulations that we can't even keep, meanwhile exalting the supernatural phenomena in his kingdom. By making the church look bad and his kingdom look exciting with all his supernatural parlor tricks he keeps people from wanting to come to church and be saved.

When the church finally accepts the supernatural lifestyle God has for us we will reveal Satan for the manipulator he really is. When the world sees the excitement and joy we have in our new lifestyles they will flock to us to hear about the love of a savior who blesses us so abundantly.

The bible says in 2 Corinthians 2:11 that we are not ignorant of Satan's devices or tactics, so let's take a look at some of his ways he uses to beat Christians off of what really belongs to them.

6 DECEPTION-SUBSTITUTION

Satan's number one weapon is deception! He is the master deceiver of all time. He could probably talk you right out of your home if you let him. Many Christians begin crying, "Do you know what the devil said and done?" When you ask them what God says they look at you in total shock as to say whom do you think you are that God would actually talk to you. Then they respond trying to be a bit spiritual, "I don't know?" They never spend time listening for the Voice of God to be manifested through the WORD OF GOD. "For such are false apostles, deceitful workers, trans- forming themselves into apostles of Christ, and no wonder! For Satan he transforms himself into an angel of light. Therefore it is no great thing if his ministers also transform themselves into ministers of righteousness, whose end will be according to their works," 2 Corinthians 11:13-15.

Many people get deceived when they rush blindly to receive greater revelation from the prophet who happens to be preaching at the local hotel that evening. Anytime some preacher tries to give you a new revelation that goes beyond the bibles teaching DON'T RECEIVE IT. I remember one particular ministry that kept sending all kinds of objects in the mail to me. I received everything from cardboard wallets that I was supposed to stuff full of money and send back to him, to empty flasks that I was sup- posed to send back to him wrapped in money. Of course the promise he would tell me is that once I sent my love offerings back to him that he would pray and God would perform some kind of miracle in my life.

Now I of all people believe in the miracle power of God, but only through the Word of God. If I saw in the Word of God that I was supposed to carry on with that kind of paraphernalia then trust me I would be in the cardboard wallet business. Mostly I would chuckle to myself when another packet of goodies would show up in the mail from this ministry. It almost became a time of fun for my wife and I as our curiosity grew with each packet sent. We would play a guessing game as to what's in the packet, coal, nails, water, etc., before we would open it. Imagine our laughter when we found coal or water with a form letter that God had given him a revelation just for us. Of course the coal represented you being a diamond in the rough and the water was from the Jordan River, and as usual a set of instructions on how many times a week you should send him money. For your convenience he would send you many Self-addressed envelopes in which to stuff full of money for him.

    Through all this fellows' foolishness one thing bothered me with every form letter he sent. He would have written out what was supposed to be a prophecy directly from the throne of God. Again, I believe in prophecy and all nine gifts of the

Holy Ghost, so prophecy doesn't bother me at all. The problem I was having was that with each packet sent the prophecy was very close to the last one. The subject or the topic of his prophecy may have varied but the intent was always the same. His prophecies were self-exalting. God, in the prophecies, was exalting him and encouraging people to send money to His servant. A major problem with that kind of prophecy is that God isn't involved in it. Anytime a man says thus saith the Lord and then goes on to exalt himself, apparently with God's approval, as though God were actually doing the speaking through him that man is in dangerous territory. God exalts people for sure, but He will not exalt me through me, He will use another person to speak well of me.

The last packet I got from that man I caught him cold. In his prophecy he made some statements that were dead wrong scripture wise. He made reference to a scripture and its contents that were totally manipulated to serve his purpose. I know because I had just finished studying that portion of scripture. The scripture stated one thing but he stated something totally different in his prophecy. I am not quick to judge any man so I wrote him a letter explaining my concerns. I never received a return to my inquiry and the packets stopped coming to my mailbox.

Deception is a subtle thing; it creeps up quietly and unexpectedly hiding in a portion of truth. It is like a good glass of orange juice to a thirsty man. The only thing is that it is laced with poison. The man will be refreshed before he dies. I came to the conclusion about this minister; that he was true and deceived or he was false and totally aware of his intentions. I will never know for sure because only God knows the true intent of that man's heart, but by operating outside of scripture he ruined any chance of help from me in helping fulfill his goals, which from my point of view was to get rich off of gullible Christians who are taught to give radically. There is absolutely nothing wrong in giving, but foolish giving is hurtful. If you're not sure about giving offerings to another ministry besides your church, ask the pastor for information about the ministry in question.

    Another area of substitution that concerns me in some of the churches I've attended is dealing with prophecy. Prophecy is good and needed in the church but Satan realizes the blessings that can come from that particular gift of the Spirit so he has a substitution that he tries to infiltrate the church with. That substitution is the spirit of divination. The spirit of divination is a religious spirit that tries to copy the voice of God in order to manipulate you through either force or pride. If you cannot be manipulated through force; as we see the apostle Paul rejoiced in his persecutions; then Satan will use pride or getting you to think more highly of yourself. Satan knows that if you get into pride you will short-circuit your

ministry and have God resist you. He found out firsthand what pride and self-exaltation does. Acts 16:16-17 "Now it happened, as we went to prayer that a certain slave girl possessed with a spirit of divination met us, who brought her masters much profit fortune-telling. This girl followed Paul and us, and cried out saying; "These men are the servants of the Most High God, who proclaim to us the way of salvation."
When you look at this prophecy at surface level you see nothing wrong with it. The apostles were servants of the Most High God and they were proclaiming the way of salvation. On the surface it looks religious and very accurate so really, what's wrong with it? This prophecy wasn't about Jesus but, it was about the men. The intent was to draw attention to the men rather than to focus attention to Jesus and the work of the cross. If that spirit of divination could get those men to agree with it and say, "YEAH, LOOK AT US," then that ministry would not be effective in reaching people for Christ.

I have had a few situations happen to me in a couple of different denominations that I associated with. In one church this lady who wore a huge cross on her neck would always interrupt the pastor in the middle of his sermon and have a word from God for him. This happened time after time. I was at that time the associate pastor of this church and was asked to talk to her about her actions. She was asked not to interrupt the service and given a pen and paper to write her words down and hand them into me to be judged. She got up in a service one morning and declared before the congregation that she would submit to the leadership. The next Sunday she was right back to doing her thing interrupting the service to bring a word for the pastor. Frustrated we just backed off for a bit and sought God on what to do. Let me clarify something at this point; my wife and I had been ordained a few months earlier and were in the process of finding our place in the five-fold ministry. Our senior pastor publicly set us in place as associate pas- tors so we could start the adventure of finding your place in the five-fold ministry. Sometimes it is an adventure because many churches and denominations recognize a one-fold ministry or two or maybe they stretch their belief system to make a three-fold ministry.

Two ministry offices that need to be restored to its fullness are the prophet's ministry and the apostle's ministry. These two ministries are looked down on because there are so many misbeliefs and little teaching on these ministries. At this time in my life I am a bi vocational minister. I work a full time job in the secular market and work full time in the church as well. I work full time to support my ministry dreams that God has laid on my heart. I was struggling with being a pastor because that wasn't the office I believe God was talking to me about, my wife agreed we are not pastor's because we don't have the mentality to put up with peoples issues who take up 90% of the pastors time and still will not change.

Back to the girl with the huge cross on her neck, I was working on the roof shingling a house when I heard this voice speak to me in my thoughts not in my heart where God usually speaks but in my thoughts. This voice told me to go to Saskatoon, I thought cool my wife and I had done a lot of work for the Lord there, winning approximately five hundred people to Jesus and held Friday night bible studies for a while. My first thought was that maybe God was going to help us renew the work we had done there ten years earlier. After a couple of days I heard this voice say go to Saskatoon again. This repeated every couple of days for about two weeks. Then one afternoon this voice spoke stronger and more forceful than before. "GO TO SASKATOON BECAUSE I JESUS SAID SO!" I recognized that forceful attitude but quite surprising the Spirit of God whispered in my heart, "Go and I will show you something and I will protect you while you go." My wife was going to Kelowna to visit her sister so I thought this would be a great time to go to Saskatoon. I traveled to Saskatoon meditating and praying all the way there, which is about ten hours from where I lived in Grande Prairie Alberta. I arrived in Saskatoon, visited a couple of friends and heard from God that going back to renew our ministry in Saskatoon was not his will for our lives. We were there for a few years in the eighties did a work for Him, completed it and now we are going to a different area to work. I traveled back to Grande Prairie and went to church the following Sunday. When I got to church the lady with the big cross on her neck came up to me and started to prophecy that I was going to become some big name Pastor and the people of Saskatoon were going to beg me to come and pastor a church in their town. Her prophecy lifted me up so high that I instantly knew which spirit her words were coming from. If I chose to follow her prophecy I knew I was headed for disaster. I decided to challenge her so I told her I thought her words were coming from the spirit of divination.

Even though she was born again and filled with the Holy Spirit she had issues in her life she needed to deal with. She grew up in an orphanage and always felt rejected or unwanted. She figured that if she flowed in the gift of prophecy and was recognized as a prophetess she then would get the recognition, attention and honor she desired. Her way to get flowing in this office and gifting was to make things up and hopefully God would bless her fabrications. Multiple guest speakers addressed her, to repent and stop making up words from God, because it is harmful and would get her into trouble. She never received correction very well and went away angry and a, "you people are judging me attitude." Later we found out her personal life was totally in disorder, she expected her husband to submit to her because she had the stronger personality and expected that she should dominate the home. She never did come back to our church but every now and then when visiting another church you see her doing the same things she was doing in our church. We also had another couple show up who were under the influence of the spirit of Jezebel. I say under the influence because I don't believe a demon spirit can possess a born again Christian. Demon spirits can influence Christians but not possess them. The husband of this couple never worked and was looking to get a position in a church setting to be able to collect a pay cheque. He would get close to someone who he thought was influential in the church and listen and memorize any prophecies that may be given to him or her by an evangelist, revivalist or guest speaker that would flow in the gifts of the Spirit. At an opportune time he would repeat this prophecy back to that person then add some of his own words to it.

We caught him red handed as my wife forgot a "p" word that an evangelist prophesied over her. This fellow got out of his chair and began to recite the prophecy this evangelist gave my wife word for word then he began to add words that were shallow and demeaning like she was a baby Christian never doing anything for God her entire life.

He seemed to forget or maybe wasn't at the ordination service when my wife and I were ordained. My wife is a natural evangelist and wins people to Jesus wherever she goes. She flows in the gifts of the Spirit and has been a great blessing to many people in the 20 years of being a Christian. My wife, Carrie, sat still but began to chuckle after the service about this fellow. We shrugged it off as foolishness and dismissed the whole thing.

We began noticing odd behavior with this couple, she would sing in a loud offensive opera style in church totally hurting the ears of people around her. When asked to tone it down a bit she would get in your face, be rude and ask you who do you think you are. Then she would ignorantly tell you that she would worship anyway God tells her to worship. Her supposed worship was the only thing that mattered. As long as she worship in her style she could care less that nobody else within ear shot could worship because of the distracting noise that came from her. She was just not carrying wrong notes or singing off key she was bad, bad, bad but had the thought she was God's gift to the musical world.

People also noticed that she would sit in the front row and began speaking word curses on our singers and worship leaders. Soon our worship team began coming down with sicknesses such as laryngitis and colds and other voice
 Effecting illnesses. While she was carrying on like this her husband began circulating throughout the congregation trying to gather people to himself as a self-proclaimed prophet. After much prayer God

show us that this couple conniving with the spirit of Jezebel was going for fame and stature in the church hoping to get wealth so they could have a relatively easy lifestyle and not have to work for a living like the rest of us.

We soon confronted this couple and all hell broke loose. They were ignorant and began demeaning the leadership of the church trying to cause dissension and get a following to join them. A few people left and followed them, but as usual the devil overplays his hand and soon he found himself by his lonesome and banned from most churches in town because repentance and submission was not found in him or his wife.

One particular service stands out in my mind with this couple. We had a joint service with three other churches and had a guest speaker come in to speak. About the middle of the service the speaker asked people to come up for prayer and a few people went up. This couple's mother went up for prayer and was apparently slain in the spirit and fell to the floor. After a couple of minutes she began to prophesy something like come on up and get the mark of God on you because the mark of the beast is coming. Okay, we watched and after about a minute her daughter began to prophecy a litter greater or intense prophecy. Then her mother who was on the floor up front began to prophesy an even bigger prophecy. I instantly knew in my spirit what was about to happen because I've seen this sort of thing in another church I attended. I turned to my wife Carrie said "look, watch what's going to happen". She turned to me and knew where my thinking was and she said, "No, no, not here." Sure enough I counted 5, 4, 3, 2, 1, then pointed to the daughter and said quietly so that only Carrie and myself could hear, "hit it." Right on cue the daughter began to prophesy a greater prophecy than the mother. I guess the mother felt conquered and couldn't beat her daughter's prophecy so she got off the floor and came back to her seat.

Later that evening when people were sitting around the alter enjoying the afterglow of the service the daughter would stare at Carrie and myself and we would notice she had no whites in her eyes. The whites of her eyes became dark like her pupils. We recognized demon activity and were not at liberty to deal with it because this couple enjoyed the demonic force that was controlling them. They were totally convinced it was God and even though you showed them scripture they would counter with scripture taken out of context and were determined they were prophets sent to bring judgment on a backslidden church. We were a part of the great falling away and they were the remnant that was going to make it to heaven. Soon this couple left our church and rumor was that they were trying to start their own church.

Another instance I am thinking of was in Bible College. I was roomed with a young fellow who seemed normal at first but after a few weeks with this fellow he started producing some bizarre behavior. When he was talking to his girlfriend on the phone he would tell her story after story about dreams, hopes and aspirations for ministry. Some of the stories were pretty wild and far out there but I just put it off to being young and trying to impress his girlfriend. I noticed no other girl in the bible college would talk to him alone without the company of others. The girls would talk to other boys in private by themselves. I began to question the girls on this and the consensus was the same. He was unsafe and untrustworthy. I decided to watch him closely and sure enough I understood why that Bible College had the nickname bridal college. Most of the young people that were there were on the make looking for prospective mates, but my roommate's reputation as a player, con artist, thief and being up on charges for rape made him a potential danger to any self-respecting women. He was later cleared of the rape charge but the appearance of evil left him in a bad spot. As time went on I began to notice him begging money off of people and even got a thousand dollars off one lady. He eventually paid her five hundred back and she soon discovered that borrowing money to this fellow was not good. He soon began to brag about being in the occult and using the spirit of divination to find out things about people. He then began to brag about being a con artist and being able to manipulate anybody into doing what he wanted. When you talked to the assistant dean about it he would just excuse it as being just young and he would grow out of it.

The thing that finally put me on edge was he asked for a copy of the poems I wrote. God has blessed me with the gifting of a psalmist. These psalms are prophetic poems from the heart of God to His people. I gave him a copy of the 40 or so poems the Lord gave me and he all of a sudden had the same gift I had, the ability to write poems.

He began to copy everything I did and he drove me nuts. During the semester break he went to Edmonton and attended some special meetings and was prophesied over that he didn't have to listen or receive teaching from man and that God was going to teach him personally. He had the idea that he was going to go sit in the Rocky Mountains by himself for a few weeks and he was going to come back with the anointing of Paul the apostle on him. He would never have to study but would get everything by divine revelation. He then would be sought after by everyone and be famous.

When challenged he would go to the assistant dean and put on this fake cry that the students became aware of and get the people who challenged him into trouble. I don't hold the Bible College staff responsible for their responding to this person's manipulation the way they did because they went home every night and never heard the lies and manipulation of this student. The students stayed at the dorms and had to tolerate this character 24 hrs a day. The staff excused it off as youth, but I called it manipulation of the spirit of divination making him think he would get fame and fortune by following that spirit. His visions that he gave people were along the same lines as the prophecy given to Paul the apostle in Acts 16:16-17. If he was truthful in operating under the influence of the spirit of divination as a non-Christian then he is susceptible to its influence as a Christian. How do you figure you might ask? Simple, this student was looking for attention, honor and accolades from other students and Bible College staff. He was very familiar with the spirit of divination and even bragged about it with a sense of wow look what I did rather than remorse for following demonic spirits. Being comfortable and even taking glory in that spirit working through him it would be easy to go back to what he is familiar and comfortable with. After all he can still walk in the lusts of his flesh and know things supernaturally from God. The spirit of divination hides in a religious cloak and you need an intimacy with Jesus to know the difference. Every soothsayer on TV and the psychic lines all believe God is giving them information not the devil.

    Prophecy is the testimony of Jesus and will exalt Jesus. By believing in a prophecy that exalts you to positions of honor and great reward where you are not in submission to anyone is setting yourself up for major hurts in your life. Remember the kingdom of God is backwards to the kingdoms world. To go up in the kingdom you first must go down or be servant of all. To get you must first give. The world is full of pride and arrogance whereas in the kingdom were commanded to be humble and not think of ourselves higher than we are. If we exalt ourselves we will be humbled. If we humble ourselves we will be exalted in due time by God. As we move closer to the coming of Jesus the devil is going to increase his efforts to stop the church from being the glorious supernatural church Jesus said it would be. If he can stop or even slow us down from being the glorious church he hopes he will slow down the time when he has a lake of fire waiting to receive him with great anticipation.

There are many false prophets in the world today promoting a gospel other than that what Christ preached. You may even find these new age prophets sitting behind a desk in schools, offices, or even involved with therapy groups. These people try to downplay the grace and power of God and encourage their philosophies, which may look good on the outside but are usually laced with poison doctrine. Continually study of the Word of God will keep you free from this kind of deception.
Cult activity is another form of deception

Satan uses to attack the church with. Cult members will usually have another book with them, which is supposedly of divine inspiration and supersedes the bible. We are to stay away from the doctrine of devils. Any new revelation outside the Word of God is a doctrine of demons.

Why do cult members carry a bible if they don't believe it? They twist scriptures and take them out of their original settings in order to promote their ideals and thus deceiving people. They have to make you believe that God is on their side. Cult members will say whatever they have to say to convince you they are the only way. Christians have been deceived by the skill of the cults in twisting scripture.

I remember reading an article where a Baptist preacher received new revelations. The article went on to say that after hearing the truth preached to him by a cult member the preacher converted to their ways. The preacher now declared that he was in the process of converting his congregation to his newfound revelations. Truth or fiction? I don't know how much confidence you can place in cult articles, but if it is true then we must be on guard against these subtle attacks. Satan is using these cults to substitute the Gospel of Christ with another gospel. Satan doesn't care what you believe in as long as it isn't the Word of God. Satan came at Jesus using the scripture so be prepared when he sends his servants to try you. Paul knew about this kind of deception when he wrote to the Galatians; "I marvel that you are turning away so soon from Him who called you in the grace of Christ, to a different gospel, which is not another; but there are some who trouble you and want to pervert the gospel of Christ. But even if we, or an angel from heaven, preach any other gospel to you, let him be accursed. As we have said before, so I now say again, if anyone preaches any other gospel to you than what you have received, let him be accursed," Galatians 1:6-9.

Don't allow the truth of God's Word to

be substituted for a watered down version of the Grace of God.

7 INTIMIDATION

Have you ever been challenged for your faith? Have people come against you violently when you've tried to witness? Do you dream of doing great things for God! Only to have people discourage you? Are you plagued with sickness and poverty? I have had all these things and worse happen to me. It took me awhile but I eventually found out why these things were happening. Satan does not like BOLD, FAITHFUL, POWERFUL CHRISTIANS. Satan likes Christians to be weak, fearful, and ineffective.

Satan uses this kind of intimidation in the natural and he uses spiritual manifestations to try and rob Christians of a glorious supernatural lifestyle.

When people start to discourage you about Jesus, turn them off quickly. You would be surprised how easily a discouraging word gets into your spirit. People, who discourage, violate the faith and confidence of their intended targets. When you are discouraged you can be easily intimidated. Words bring life or they bring death, discouragers speak words of death and failure. Encouragers speak words of life and success. Make your company among those who encourage you to succeed and avoid the discouragers at all costs.

    If Satan cannot intimidate you through other people he may try the supernatural to beat you. I have heard testimonies where demons have manifested themselves to people and sought to destroy them. I have had dreams where I came under demonic attack; they would show up in my house in a dream and try to hurt me. After about two weeks a physical manifestation of the spiritual attack would manifest. I learned two take these types of dreams seriously and put on the armor of God when they happened. My ignorance of the meaning of these types of dreams almost cost me my life. Most people would react to this form of manifestation in fear and terror. That my fellow Christian is exactly what the devil wants you to do. Satan knows the moment you get into fear, your Christian life becomes paralyzed and you are easily beaten. You do not have to live in fear no matter how violently Satan comes against you. BE OF GOOD COURAGE for Jesus has set us free from the power of Satan.

Let me share our victory in this area. It all began when our clocks began to work by themselves without the aid of batteries. Our bedroom door would open and close by itself and strange noises could be heard in our house in the middle of the night. Every time these things would happen, a blanket of fear would settle in our house. Finally it all came to a head when we fled our home after a mirror lifted off our dresser and smashed against the floor. When I heard a voice threaten my life, as I was going to pick up the pieces, we decided it was time to leave.

We ran to a friend's house seeking refuge. The next morning our friend shared with us on how to overcome fear and the devil. What we didn't know is that fear will cause satanic manifestations; in the same way faith will cause Godly manifestations! We began to study the bible to find out what victory Jesus provided for us concerning fear. We were quite relieved when we were taught to resist the devil and could have victory in our lives.

That evening we went home armed with the Word of God and our faith. The blanket of fear rolled on into our house at bedtime as it had so many times before. Before it could settle and cause manifestations we attacked it with the Word of God. We read scriptures by the score, in fact we had about ninety scriptures, reminding the spirit of fear of the victory Jesus provided for us. We would not tolerate his presence in our house and lives anymore. Needless to say, within half an hour the peace of God settled in and we were sound asleep.

Another episode happened while I was at my father in-law's house sharing Jesus with him. Upon arriving home at eleven o'clock my wife Carrie proceeded to share her experience with me. Shortly after I had left to visit with her father she noticed the cat standing at the top of the basement stairs. The cat was acting very strange, his fur was sticking straight up and he was hissing violently. Now this was unusual for this cat to do that because he was one of those tabbies who would eat and sleep not caring about anything going on around him. To watch this cat chase a mouse you would have thought they were best buddies.

The cat then took off running in the other direction. Carrie sensed a strange presence entering the house. To Carrie's surprise the presence moved down the hallway and into our bedroom. Carrie ran to the bedroom after she heard our king size water bed sloshing around to find our blankets messed up and thrown in disarray on the bed. Having put up with enough from this spirit she rebuked it in Jesus name and told it to leave. The spirit left but my wife was ticked over the fact that some dumb demon had the audacity to come into our house and mess up our bed. We later realized that this was the tactic of the devil to try to get Carrie into fear and to call me home. The devil did not want me witnessing to her father. Carrie knew and understood her authority in Christ and could handle the devil by herself.

By knowing your authority in Christ you can have victory over Satan, whether he tries to manifest in the natural or spiritual realm. You don't have to be fearful or intimidated, we have **VICTORY**.

"Be sober, be vigilant; because your adversary the devil walks about like a roaring lion, seeking whom he may devour, resist him, steadfast in the faith, knowing that the same sufferings are experienced by your brotherhood in the world," 1 Peter 5:8-9.

Intimidation may increase against the

church but doesn't fear for we have authority over the devil and nothing shall harm us, Luke 10:19. It is time that we walk free of these hindrances and intimidations and move on into the supernatural. Let us cast off the cares of life, live repentant lives, walk in the light free of deception, resist the devil with all our might and seek after the knowledge of God. Here are four areas every Christian should know if he (she) wishes to walk victorious.
1) What happened to us when we were born again? 2) What we now are in Christ Jesus. 3) What we now have in Christ Jesus. 4) The authority we now have in Christ Jesus.

Jesus said in John 10:10 that He came to give us abundant life. Arise church and go on into the abundant supernatural life Jesus provides for us.

8 REVEALING OF SIN

Many times God will talk through a dream or vision. His desire is to instruct the Body of Christ especially in these latter times. Job 33:14-18 says that God speaks to us and seals our instructions when deep sleep falls upon us while slumbering in our beds. Acts 2:16–21 speaks of God giving dreams and visions to His people in these times. As each year brings us closer to the second coming of Jesus, visions and dreams are going to increase in the church.

This next dream I am going to share has some similarities to the dream I have shared in the previous chapter. Though there are similarities the message of the dream is different, yet important.

This dream began a bit differently than the previous dream. In the last dream I was involved in it. In this dream I was not directly involved in the activities. It was as if I was on the outside looking in. I was watching the events unfold before me through what seemed like a picture frame or a window.

As I looked in I could see religious people all around. These people were quite active in their assigned duties. To the right of the main group I noticed a few people leave the camp and head through the bush in a south direction. In the dream I followed those who left the camp to a road. On this road a military jeep drove up with commandos in it. It was obviously an enemy to these people because the soldiers began shooting at them seeking to destroy the religious people. Wounded and bleeding they escaped and made their way back to the camp.

As they entered the camp, evening was starting to set in; people were finishing their work and getting ready to retire for the rest of the night. Just before night could settle in strange things began to happen. The earth began to shake and stars began to fall from heaven. As I looked toward the east my spirit leaped within me. The Holy Spirit was on the move again. Everybody in the dream began to rise off the ground; no one was left on the ground. People began to rise higher and higher but some people stopped at approximately fifteen feet, while others continued to go higher until they were out of sight.

The people who only rose fifteen feet began to turn in circles. As they turned in circles I became aware of everything about them. There was nothing that could be hidden as they continued to revolve in a complete 360-degree circle.

Watching with interest I asked the Lord, "Lord what is this, what is happening?" the Spirit of God responded, "This is the revealing of sin." After a couple of minutes the dream ended.

This dream happened a couple of weeks after the dream we spoke of in the last chapter. These two dreams were connected in some way but I couldn't get a grasp on them. When the Lord spoke the words repentance before resurrection to me the second dream became clear to me as well.

The camp full of religious people represented the Body of Christ, the Church or the household of God. The assigned duties represented the calling and work that God has placed upon His Church. The people represented minis- tries as well as individuals. These people were faithfully doing the work of the ministry assigned to them by the Holy Spirit, or so it seemed. The people who wandered off through the bushes rep- resent individuals and ministries who have gotten off into rebellion and decided to go and do things their own way. This is typical of many denominations today that reject the Holy Ghost and His manifestations. "There is a way which seems right to a man, but its end is the way of death," Proverbs 14:12. As these individuals and ministries continue along their own paths, Satan will be ready and waiting for them. The jeep full of military personnel represented this. Satan will seek to kill, destroy and steal big time from these people. Satan will make sure that this group of people will have major media attention in order to discredit the true Church of God. The jeep and guns of the military in comparison to the unarmed people who were walking, represents Satan's power over those in rebellion. They will be powerless to resist the devil because of the rebellion and pride in their own abilities, which engulf their hearts. Wounded and defeated they will return to the household of God.

The part about evening setting in signifies the close of the church age. Before the Church Age comes to a close we are going to see a move of God so intense that the earth and stars will be drastically affected. Jesus is coming back for His people with power and Glory. As in the previous dream people began to lift off the ground. They were being lifted to a supernatural life. Some could not go on into the supernatural life because of **unrepentant sin in their**

lives. The fact that they stayed hovering above the ground turning inn circles showed the futility of hiding things from God. God knows and sees all things. God desires to have a clean church, pure and holy unto Himself. In this hour we see God moving to bring His people to repentance. The Bible says in Isaiah 26:9 that when the judgments of God are in the earth, men will know

Righteousness. God's desire is for your best. We will not attain to His best for our lives with sin laden unrepentant hearts. The Bible says that judgment begins with the house of God. God is continually cleaning out the sin in His Church.

We can deal with sin in one of two ways; confess and repent and turn away from sin or hide our sin, deny it and claim innocence. What way do you wish to go? Personally I would rather confess and repent and by confess I mean name THE SIN AND TAKE PERSONAL OWNERSHIP OF IT rather than generalize it and put it off as a mere inconvenience, when I know I've done wrong. It is easier on my emotions and physical body to repent before sin becomes a stronghold in my life.

"He who covers his sin will not prosper, but whoever confesses and forsakes them will have mercy," Proverbs 28:13.

"Poverty and shame will come to him who disdains correction, but he who regards reproof will be honored," Proverbs 28:13.

The above versus bring to remembrance two ministers I know of. One minister tried to hide the sin he indulged in, saying that he never knew he did wrong. Even in the light of overwhelming evidence he kept denying his guilt. Finally he ended up in jail and spent a few years paying for his sins. Thank God he realized his errors and now after being free from prison we see the mercy of God at work by restoring this man to ministry again. The other minister had to be dealt with in a harsh manner as well. He would not confess his sin, even after a fellow minister confronted him on it, so his sin was revealed to the whole world. When his sin became known, rather than deny his involvement, he confessed it before the public. He then asked for forgiveness from the Body of Christ and is in the process of honoring the correction and reproof brought upon him by the Lord. This man shall surely be restored to his ministry once again because of the love and mercy of God the Father.

"And be sure your sin will find you out," Numbers 32:32b.

Satan will target ministries and people that are in the public eye, if there are some skeletons in the closet, mainly to bring disorientation and disrespect to the church. What about the individuals who are not in the public eye? Unrepentant sin will affect you and your family and cause disorientation and rifts between family members. Indulging in sinful habits, cause you to become blind and stupid to the blessings of God.

God had spoken to the children of Israel and gave them a command to fill. He warned them that if they were not obedient then it would be sin to them. He told them that their sin would surely find them out. This principle still applies to the New Testament people as well. In the New Testament we see evidence of sin finding out people. "But a certain man named Ananias, with Sapphira his wife, sold a possession. And he kept back part of the proceeds, his wife also being aware of it, and brought a certain part and laid it at the Apostles feet. But Peter said, "Ananias why has Satan filled your heart to lie to the Holy Spirit and keep back part of the price of the land for yourself?" "While it remained was it not your own? And after it was sold, was it not in your own control? You have not lied to men but to God." Then Ananias, hearing these words, fell down and breathed his last. Great fear came upon all those who heard these things. And the young men arose and wrapped him up,

carried him out, and buried him. Now it was about three hours later when his wife came in, not knowing what had happened. And Peter answered her, "Tell me whether you sold the land for so much?" and she said, "Yes for so much." Then Peter said to her, "How is it that you have agreed together to test the Spirit of the Lord? Look at the feet of those who have buried your husband is at the door, and they will carry you out." Then
Immediately she fell down at his feet and breathed her last. And the young men came in and found her dead, fear came upon all the Church and upon all who heard these things," Acts 5:1-11.

  Ananias and Sapphira paid a heavy price for indulging in sin when the supernatural power of God was poured out. As believers we cannot indulge in sin and stand in the presence of almighty God. When the supernatural power of God is being manifested mightily, sin in our lives will short- circuit our life. Why do you think we don't see a stronger move of the Spirit of God in our churches today? We must come to a place of repentance before God. **"REPENTANCE BEFORE RESURRECTION."**

We are in the last of the last days. We are about to see the greatest outpouring of the supernatural resurrection power of God on this earth. This outpouring will be greater than anything ever experienced in the history of mankind.
God is warning us that this spiritual explosion is about to take place. If God didn't warn us and prepare us for this event, our churches would be full of dead bodies. The spiritual explosion is going to come from God using the Church as His channel or vessels to carry that explosion to the lost. That much power when short-circuited by sin could cause the demise of the vessel the power is flowing through. God wants a church without spot or wrinkle. He does not want a church full of

dead people. Either we confess the sin in our lives so that God can cleanse us and release us from it or He will reveal it for all to see. The bottom line of the dream is that sin and rebellion is coming out of the church one way or the other. We should be living repented lives before God. God said, "Be holy even as I am Holy," 1Peter 1:16. Turn the world off and turn on to Jesus. Now most Christians don't deliberately try to walk in sin, but we do slip up. When you realize you've sinned in any area of your life, confess it before God and repent of the sin before it becomes habitual. When sin becomes habitual, Satan will use it to build strong holds in your life. His goal is to lead you into destruction. A man who is quick to repent before God will have mercy. "If we confess our sins, He is faithful and just to forgive us our sins and to cleanse us from all unrighteousness," 1John 1:9.

    When sin finds a foothold in your life be sure that it will bring some of its friends with it. Sickness and disease, depression, confusion and emotional torment are but a few friends to sin. It is easier on a person's physical body and emotions to be cleansed of sin immediately rather than carry sin and its many friends around with us. Sin will place a heavy burden on your life if you allow it to go unchecked.

The Spirit of God taught me how to live a repentant life. The Lord started me off with a simple but effective prayer: "Lord reveal to me the sin in my life so I can confess it, repent of it, and be cleansed by the Blood of Christ, so there is nothing between you and me that would hinder our communication and relationship. I prayed this prayer continually. Soon the Lord began to show areas of my life, which needed cleansing by the blood. As the Lord showed me each area I would confess the sin, repent of it and receive the cleansing from unrighteousness. One area the Lord showed me I had to deal with was blasphemy. Don't get freaked out or judgmental on that statement, let me explain. When the Lord told me to repent of blasphemy I needed understanding because I am not one for curse words or using God's name in vain in the way most of us understand it. He showed me that when a person uses His name in a joking manner or hold it as common as any other name it is really blasphemy to Him. Jehovah, Jesus, Holy Spirit, are names that are Holy and powerful and should be spoken with reverence rather than light hearted and common.

    One day in my prayer time my spirit began to trouble me. I knew there was sin blocking my spirit from receiving from God. I asked the Lord to show me the sin that was blocking me. He did. As He revealed each sin I would confess it and be cleansed. Then the Lord brought up one particular sin and I thought, "**NO WAY**." I told the Lord, "You must have made a mistake because I don't remember doing that." I know the Holy Spirit doesn't make mistakes but I couldn't remember the incident He was referring to. I asked Jesus to show me exactly, without a shadow of a doubt what I had done wrong. To my surprise a vision unfolded before me. In this vision I could see every detail; where I was sitting, my conversation, and the expression on my face. I could even hear my thoughts as people went by our table in the restaurant. The sin the Lord was talking about happened earlier that day at a restaurant. It wasn't a sin that manifested itself in the natural but a sin that was a strong hold in my thought life. Talk about removing all doubt, here I was watching myself and hearing the sinful thoughts I was entertaining that day. Confessing that sin came quickly as I realized that God hears you're thought audibly. Nothing is hid from God.

"Nevertheless the solid foundation of God stands, having this seal: "The Lord knows those who are His," and, "Let everyone who names the name of Christ depart from iniquity." But in a great house there are not only vessels of gold and silver, but also of wood and clay, some for honor and some for dishonor. Therefore if anyone cleanses himself from the latter, he will be a vessel for honor, sanctified and useful for the master, prepared for every good work. Flee also youthful lusts; but pursue righteousness, faith, love, peace, with those who call on the Lord out of a pure heart,"

    2 timothy 2:19-22.

**AMAZING GRACE HOW SWEET THE
SOUNDS BECAUSE OF LOVE THAT KNOWS
NO BOUNDS I WAS LOST IN SIN AND
UNDONE
REDEEMED THRU THE CROSS OF YOUR
ONLY SON
GRACE CAME WITH BLESSINGS BY THE
SCORE JESUS STANDS KNOCKING AT MY
HEART'S DOOR WILL I LET THE RIGHTEOUS
ONE IN
TO SAVE AND REDEEM FROM THE POWER
OF SIN
HOSANNA IN THE HIGHEST, HOLY, HOLY,
HOLY ONE I RECEIVE YOU IN MY HEART,
JESUS THE SON BECAUSE OF GRACE YOU
WERE RAISED
FOREVER NOW TO BE PRAISED**

9 WORDS

Words! It is totally amazing that this subject is probably one of the most taught subjects yet, the Body of Christ is still grossly ignorant of the effect words have in our lives. It is time to wake up and realize what is happening here. In the following dream we are going to see the importance and power of words and why Satan would like to control your tongue.

This dream started with my wife Carrie and I walking up the sidewalk on our way to church. Upon entering the lobby of the church we noticed the Pastor standing a few feet inside the sanctuary. We thought this was rather strange as the pastor was usually in the lobby greeting people. The pastor was bidding people to come into the sanctuary and take a seat. The look on the pastor's face was very different than the joyful expression he usually carted around. You could see fear in his eyes and a slight trembling of his body. I was wondering why the other people who were filing into the sanctuary were totally oblivious to the pastor's nervous apprehension. Soon the entire congregation was seated. The pastor made his way to the pulpit and began to speak. About a minute into the pastor's message a sound echoed throughout the sanctuary. The sound was the sound of rifle bolts being snapped into place arming the weapons. I turned around to see the source of the sound. In the balcony of our church were people holding guns of all kinds. They were carrying rifles, shotguns, machine guns, and a variety of other high-powered weapons. This group of people was holding the entire church captive. There were only a few gunmen but the entire congregation sat in fear of these men. These men told the congregation to sit quietly or else they would be shot. I looked around the church and everyone was paralyzed with fear.

     Suddenly I began to quote scriptures from the bible. I quoted Isaiah 54:17, "No weapon formed against you shall prosper, and every tongue which raises against you in judgment you shall condemn. This is the heritage of the servants of the Lord, and their righteousness is from me, says the Lord." I also quoted Luke 10:19, "Behold, I give you the authority to trample on serpents and scorpions, and over all the power of the enemy, and nothing shall by any means hurt you."

I quoted these scriptures three or four times, and then I stood to my feet. Turning to face our captors, I continued quoting scriptures. The gunmen started shouting and hollering for me to sit down and shut up or else I would be shot. I use the term gunmen here in a most generic term not implying just males but including females in the term as well. I started to make my way to the balcony still quoting scriptures. I yelled the scriptures so loud, in response to their threats that I blocked out the sounds they were making.

    These scriptures exploded in my heart becoming so powerful and overwhelmed me to the degree that the truths they portrayed became the only thing I could comprehend or understand.

The gunmen opened fire upon me with every weapon they had. I kept quoting Isaiah 54:17 and Luke 10:19 as the bullets bounced off my chest. The men were really surprised to see that their weapons had no effect on me. I proceeded to the balcony, disarmed them, and brought them down to the front of the church.

The pastor started preaching with enthusiasm and fire from the core of his being as the gunmen were coming down the aisle toward the front of the church. When the gunmen got to the front of the church the pastor became unglued, preaching with everything he had in him. The Anointing of God was released and after a few minutes some of the gun- men broke down and repented for their actions against the church. When we enquired of the remaining gunmen as to whether or not they would like to repent demonic spirits began to manifest through them. We commanded the devils to leave in the name of Jesus Christ. After the devils left the remaining gunmen repented. This was the end of the dream.

The interpretation of the dream is this; the gunmen are Christians, the rifles and high-powered weapons are the Christian's tongues; the bullets are **WORDS.** The Christians in the balcony represent their position of spirituality they thought they had attained. They believed they were greater in their walk with God than anyone else. They exalted themselves above measure simply because they had an office or a position or title in the church. Their words brought fear and bondage upon all who heard them speak in the church. This was easily accomplished by having the congregation believe their exalted position.

When I stood up and challenged them they felt threatened, unleashing words meant for my destruction. The scriptures I quoted not only protected me but also disarmed them. These people were using their tongues to control the church. By creating an atmosphere of fear and bondage the church remained paralyzed. The Holy Spirit wasn't able to move the way He wanted to in this church because when He would move He be spoken against, especially if it wasn't the way the gunmen thought it should be. The Holy Spirit is a gentleman and will not include us in His moves if we don't want to be involved. He will pass over us and let us have our fear and bondage if we want it. After being brought down from their lofty perch, they were escorted to the front of the church. The pastor preached God's word with authority and power because he himself was set free when these people were removed from their lofty perch. After hearing the Word of God many repented while others had to have the devil cast off of them. Once the devil was gone then all could repent and be set free from their patterns of destruction they were causing.

I believe and have seen this sort of activity happening in many churches today. Some of the people who use their tongues for destruction are simply ignorant of the harm they are doing. When they are quiet long enough to hear God's voice manifested through His Word they will repent. You may have to challenge them to change. We also have those who are so caught up with religion and tradition that blind- ness has come upon them in part. This type of people looks to the past. When God moved a certain way back then and they had an experience with Him they seem to think that that is the only way God moves and speak against any new thing He may be attempting to do in their church. They like their comfort zones and continually thwart the plan of God by using demeaning destructive words to stop the move of God in their church.

Then there are those who are under the control of evil spirits. These people need to be delivered from this devilish activity. In one church I attended, a situation similar to the dream presented itself. I met this young lady who seemed very spiritual. Her husband also seemed quite stable in his walk with the Lord. It wasn't until about one month later that the true state of their spiritual walk surfaced. This young woman lived in a state of fear. She believed her husband was doing every immoral sex act imaginable with both male and female companions. She attacked him continually with her words. Her words were very destructive and demeaning. Their marriage was falling apart rapidly. After talking with her husband we found out he was not the pervert she said he was. He had even attempted to get counseling from the pastor of their church over this situation. Another sad thing I dis- covered was that she would attack his friends with her tongue, blaming them that they were participants.

Satan had this girl so convinced she was right that she would not listen to anyone who opposed her words. All the counseling and sharing the Word of God fell on deaf ears. She would become excited if you agreed with her accusations. Satan began to use her to speak words of strife and fear amongst church members. Some people began to agree with her while others would not. She was causing a rift in the church and she seemed to enjoy doing it. At times we would sit with this couple, over a cup of coffee, and share with her on how the devil controls your tongue if you would let him. She would agree with us that those things were so but also assure us that this was not the case with her. She would never allow us to pray with her to set her free because she enjoyed the way she lived. Soon she got to the point where she could not tolerate people who had good marriages. She began to plant words of distrust and fear into couples; trying to prove their marriages was not good. Subconsciously she wanted every marriage to be like hers, and if they were not she would try to change them. When she began to accuse my wife of immoral acts with her husband, we felt it was time to break off any kind of friend-ship we had with that couple. This woman would not accept help from us in any way.

After the relationship with this girl was terminated we were still harassed over the phone for many months. This girl phoned people we associated with asking them to pray for us because she thought we were caught up in immorality. Actually she was looking for someone to validate her words so as to not look like a fool when she was to be confronted. You would be surprised or maybe not how much malicious gossip is spread amongst Christians under the guise of prayer. It wasn't until we took authority over Satan, who was operating through her, that the accusations stopped.

When people come across your path that is bent on speaking words of destruction, stay away from them. By taking authority over Satan and using scripture you can stop the evil words right in their tracks. You don't have to be a victim of other people's tongues. Satan loves to find someone who will give him control of his or her tongues. He can use these people to steal from, kill and destroy other Christians. Satan was able to work through this lady because she very seldom prayed and spent very little time in the Word of God. When you don't pray or read the bible, how do you expect to have the Amour of God on when the devil tries to influence you? Having on the Armor of God on protects you from the attacks of the devil. Don't be deceived when people bring demeaning words to attack you remember our warfare is not with flesh and blood but with spiritual forces. Satan is merely using that persons tongue to hurt you as much as possible.

    Another experience that helped me out in this area was in a church I recently stopped attending. We usually have a prayer meeting Wednesday night and this particular night while I was praying in the Spirit I could hear the sound of metal clanging together. I soon had revelation that the Armor of God was being put on me and I initially though wow God is going to take us into some heavy spiritual battles. To my surprise the meeting was cut short and most of the people went down stairs for refreshments, leaving the pastor and myself to talk. After a short conversation about nothing the pastor began to belittle me calling me a false prophet saying that none of my prophecies came to pass and that I was out to destroy his church. After he was finished his tirade I explained to him on how prophecies given to people were conditional and how he began to sabotage each prophecy given because they never glorified him, and my- self as well as others noticed he would intimidate anyone who had a stronger personality and anointing on them than he had. I had given him and his wife teaching on the prophetic simply because a good majority of the congregation was prophetic and really needed some teaching in this area.

They never looked at the material I gave them and just pushed everything away. I was glad I had on the Armor of God or I would have been affect by that tirade. I remembered the scripture God gave me as a ten year old boy,
The scripture was Ezekiel 3:10-11, "Moreover He said to me: "Son of man, receive into your heart all my words that I speak to you, and hear with your ears. And go, get to the captives, to the children of your people, and speak to them and tell them, 'Thus says the Lord God,' whether they hear, or whether they refuse."

    With the Armor of God on I never took offense. I realized he had the issues and that by taking offense I would be falling into the trap Satan was setting for me. "Finally, my brethren, be strong in the Lord, and in the power of His might. Put on the whole Armor of God, that ye may be able to stand against the wiles of the devil, Ephesians 6:10-24.

10 GOD SEES OUR WORDS AS POWERFUL INSTRUMENTS

Death and life are in the power of the tongue, and those who love it will eat its fruit." Proverbs 18:21.

Do you use your tongue to promote life or death? When people look at you do they know you as an encourager or a discourager? Do you lift people up? Do you tear people down? Remember God is not mocked; a man will reap what he sows. When you encourage others then others will encourage you. Promote life not death!!

Proverbs is a book about wisdom, let's check and see how important words are in this book.

"My son, give attention to my words; incline your ear to my sayings. Do not let them depart from your eyes; keep them in the midst of your heart; for they are life to those who find them, and health to all their flesh. Keep your heart with all diligence, for out of it spring the issues of life. Put away from you a deceitful mouth, and put perverse lips far from you," Proverbs 4:20-24.

"These six things the Lord hates, yes, seven are an abomination to him: A proud look, a LYING TONGUE, hands that shed innocent blood, a heart that devises wicked plans, feet that are swift in running to evil, a false witness who SPEAKS LIES, and one who sows discord among brethren," Pr. 6:16-19.

"You are snared by the words of your own mouth; you are taken by the words of your mouth," Proverbs 6:2.

"Listen, for I will speak of excellent things, and from the opening of my lips will come right things; for my mouth will SPEAK TRUTH; wickedness is an abomination to my lips. All the words of my mouth are righteousness; nothing crooked or perverse is in them," Proverbs 8:6-8.

"The fear of the Lord is to hate evil; pride and arrogance and the evil way and the perverse mouth I hate," Proverbs 8:13.

God wants us to speak words of truth! What are words of truth? Words of truth are those words, which line up with God's Word. Words that edify, uplift, strengthen, and encourage others to seek after the ways of the Lord are words of truth. Words of truth are those words, which line up with the covenant promises of God, especially in the face of contrary circumstances.

Wicked, lying, and perverse words are to be put far from us. What are wicked, lying, and perverse words? Words that demean, destroy, discourage and take away from the truths of God's Word; or from your relationship with the Lord are wicked, lying, and perverse words.

Truthful speaking is very important in order to walk successfully in the supernatural manifestations of God. Words play an important part in our daily lives. You can honestly say, "MY life is governed by my words." What you were saying yesterday is what you are walking today. Your life will never rise above the words you speak.

Some people I know live atrocious lives as Christians and justify he or herself, by saying God knows my heart. The bible says that we are going to be judged for everything good or bad that we do in the body and that Jesus is coming back to reward us for our works. Out of the abundance of the heart the mouth speaks and we usually always walk our talk. So we can see the heart condition by our words and actions. We need to come to a place where we realize the seriousness of spoken words; how they affect others and ourselves. Let us repent for the wicked words we speak.

    People who decide to become an edifier and encourager will experience the supernatural. God can trust them to speak His Words over every situation continually. God can trust these people with His power. They seek to lift people above the pressures of life. God is a "People person." Become a people person and watch God move through your life to strengthen and uplift others. The supernatural power of God will flow through you. REPENT AND GET READY FOR POWER.

THE ENCOURAGER

Who is this one who brings encouragement?
Obviously one whom heaven has sent
She reaches out when others are down
Imparting hope and smiles in the place of a frown
Who is this one from whom strength flows
On her my anointing continually glows
Bringing joy and peace to all her peers
She reaches out to wipe their tears
To my child I shall say
My peace on you shall continually stay
To the one who looks to others best?
Enter thou into my holy rest

11 THE SUPERNATURAL FLOOD OF GOD

Enter into His gates with thanksgiving, and into His courts with praise. Be thankful to Him, and bless His name," Psalm 100:4. While visiting my cousin Lori one summer afternoon we decided to obey Psalm 100:4. After spending a fair amount of time in praise and worship the presence of God manifested. A very high piercing sound went off in my spirit. The whistling sound was so loud I could almost hear it with my physical ears. The sound was meant to get my attention.

A very interesting vision burst forth into my spirit. I watched as waves of the ocean rolled into shore. I didn't notice anything strange or different about how the waves came in. they just rolled in and receded, only to be caught up with an incoming wave. I watched as four or five waves made their way into shore in the same manner. Finally the last wave of the series hit the shore and began to recede.

Something different was happening. There was not another wave coming in to meet the one receding. Instead, the wave continued to recede, revealing the ocean floor. The ocean floor was beautiful. Nothing was out of place and it was clean. You could find nothing rotting or decaying. It was actually amazing as to the cleanliness of the ocean floor. The way the wave was receding I thought someone was draining the ocean.

Suddenly, after what seemed like half the ocean floor was uncovered, the wave began to make its way back to shore. I noticed something very different about this wave as it came in. this incoming wave was many, many times bigger than all the others. The wave was so huge it was like the entire ocean was rolling into shore at once. It moved toward the shore faster and faster. As the wave picked up velocity the earth began to tremble and shake. The thunderous roar from this wave was almost deafening. As the wave got closer I became excited in my spirit. I could see Jesus riding the crest of this wave. I watched as the wave was coming into shore at breakneck speed. Then just as quick as it started, the vision ended.

I pondered these visions and dreams in my heart for many years. All these experiences mentioned up to this place took place well before 1987. It is exciting when God reveals situations and moves of His Spirit to you and you watch them being fulfilled before your very eyes.

This vision is tied in with the others. The same day the Lord said repentance before resurrection, this vision opened up as well. The waves of the ocean represent moves of God in the earth. The seashore represents humanity. The ocean floor represents the church of the Living God. Basically here is what's happening; the church is the vehicle, which carries the move of God to the rest of humanity. God uses the church as His vehicle to reach lost people. All through history we see God moving in different waves of His Glory restoring truths and gifts to the body of Christ. With each move of God multiple thousands have come to the saving knowledge of Jesus Christ. God has been preparing the la- borers to work in His vineyard to get ready for the great harvest yet to come.

God has been preparing the Body of Christ for a long time. Preparing her for what you might ask? To be the vehicle which can carry the fullness of His Glory to the earth? When the fullness of His Glory manifests we will see a harvest of souls into His kingdom greater than we've ever seen before.

The ocean floor was clean and pure representing the state that the church is going to be in when the big wave hits. The wave that receded far out into the ocean, revealing the ocean floor, is a wave of holiness and judgment leading to repentance in which I believe the church is now involved in. Brother Kenneth Hagin prophesied that 2005 is going to be the year that God was going to judge His Church. Could 2005 be the beginning of the cleansing wave of God to His Church?

"The way of the just is uprightness; O Most Upright, You weigh the path of the just. Yes, in the way of your judgments, O Lord, we have waited for you; the desire of our soul is Your Name and for the remembrance of you. With my soul I have desired you in the night, Yes, by my spirit within me I will seek you early; for when your judgments are in the earth, the inhabitants of the world will learn righteousness," Isaiah 26:7-9.

"For the time has come for judgment to begin at the house of God; and if it begins with us first, what will be the end of those who do not obey the Gospel of God? Now, if the righteous one is scarcely saved, where will the ungodly and the sinner appear?" 1Peter4: 17-18

The word judgment in Isaiah is the Hebrew word "Mishpat" which means a verdict pronounced, a sentence or formal decree, a right, or privilege, determination, and discretion. The word judgment in 1 Peter is the Greek word "krino" which means to distinguish, decide, to try, decree, determine, esteem, call in question, sentence to, and think, the function or the affect for or against.

From these two meanings I see that God is going to look into the practices we have as Churches and church members and determine if they are upright before God or have we strayed so far and been lulled to sleep by the world. I believe once God has scrutinized our lives and churches then we are going to see His decrees and determinations. Either we are going to be on the good or blessing side of Judgment or it's time for God to do some major discipline to His Body. I would rather live a repentant life style and be found seeking our Father in Heaven when judgment comes, than living a carefree, backslidden, rebellious life and be taken to God's woodshed for some major discipline. The bottom line ladies and gentlemen is that sin is going to come out of God's camp once and for all. God's love for us is too great not to purify us and help us. I guess the question you have to ask yourself is, "Am I going to live a repentant lifestyle and be on my face continually before God? Or am I going to continue rebellion and test God to see if He has the nerve to take me to the woodshed and straighten me up or is He going to let me walk in my own rebellious ways, which will ultimately produce death in me.

The big wave represents the resurrection power of the Holy Spirit about to be released to this planet. Jesus riding the crest represents the closing of the church age. This wave of power will bring

Jesus back for the church. The resurrection of the church is at hand! This move of the power of God will be so powerful and all-consuming that no one will be able to stand against it. The only way to move with this wave is to ride the crest and allow it to draw you into the supernatural. This wave of the Holy Ghost will usher us into the very presence of Almighty God. Resisting this move of the Spirit will prove to be futile. God can only control this wave. Anyone found resisting this flood of spiritual power would be swept away. If you find this hard to believe try stopping a natural tidal wave. Man has not accomplished this. How much greater is the spiritual world, since the physical world is controlled by the spiritual world.

The wave of supernatural power is coming through the church. The ocean floor or church is free from all hindrances enabling this wave to increase in speed. This wave will pick up speed as it races through the church. A pure, repentant, washed in the blood, church will receive this supernatural power. This move of the Holy Ghost will continue through the church, picking up velocity, until it bursts on a dying world. The supernatural signs and wonders brought on by this wave will usher millions into the kingdom of Heaven. This wave will engulf entire cities at once. Nothing will escape the effects of this wave of power. This flood of power will affect all flesh on earth.

Let us prove from the Bible that this spiritual flood is on the way. "But (instead) this is (the beginning of) what was spoken through the prophet Joel: And it shall come to pass in the last days, God declares, that I will pour out of my Spirit upon all mankind, and your sons and daughters shall prophecy [telling forth the divine counsels] and your young men shall see visions (divinely granted appearances), and your old men shall dream [divinely suggested] dreams. Yes, and on my menservants also on my handmaidens in those days I will pour out of my Spirit, and they shall prophecy [telling forth the divine counsels and predicting future events pertaining especially to God's kingdom]. And I will show wonders in the sky above and signs on the earth beneath, blood and fire and smoking vapor: The sun shall be turned into darkness and the moon into blood before the obvious day of the Lord comes – that great and notable and conspicuous and renowned [day]. And it shall be that whoever shall call upon the name of the Lord [invoking, adoring, and worshipping the Lord Christ] shall be saved," Acts 2:16-21, Amplified Bible, see Joel 2:28-32.

We are about to experience the greatest outpouring of the Glory of God in the history of mankind. What is the purpose? In verse 21 the conclusion to the previous verse is known, salvation!

    Acts 2:16-21 is not a scripture dealing

with the tribulation period as so many people think. It is dealing with the church age. Peter, at the day of Pentecost, gave a reference to the event that was taking place; this is the beginning and not the fulfillment. This scripture will be fulfilled at the close of the church age.

You will notice Acts 2:17 says, "And it shall come to pass in the last days." The beginning of the last days began at the birth of the church on the day of Pentecost. The people experienced a supernatural outpouring of the Holy Ghost at their birth. So shall we experience a supernatural outpouring when the church graduates and is caught up into Glory. Peter saw the beginning; you and I shall see the end. The church came to the earth in supernatural power and it will leave in like manner. I believe that we may very well be the generation that shall see the fulfillment of Acts 2.

We are moving closer and closer to the coming of Christ for His church. Bible prophecy is being fulfilled rapidly. The power of God is being demonstrated on a larger scale. We are on a countdown to power. God is not short on mercy or grace but He is short on time. The heavenly Father has allotted a certain amount of time for the restoration of all things. We have 6,000 years behind us and the seventh day or millennium just ahead of us. We are in a little sliver of compressed time to see the harvest of the righteous from the earth. Revival is starting to break out in many places on the earth. God's healing power is flowing. The gifts of the Holy Spirit are in greater manifestation. The last statistics I read declared that 250,000 people a week were coming to Jesus.

Churches who reject the manifestations of the Holy Spirit will suffer tremendous losses. The churches that move on with God, being current and not old and antiquated, encourage their members to seek God and allow the manifestations of the Holy Spirit, will experience the greatest influx of new converts. These churches will grow strong and become powerful vessels, which God will use to reach the lost.

"I will show wonders in Heaven above and signs in the earth beneath: blood and fire and vapor of smoke," Acts 2:19.

We are about to experience a return to the signs that God has said should follow the believer. These signs have not left the church, but you have to travel for miles to find a church where they manifest. Signs in the church should be as common as houses to live in. if there are no signs being manifested in your church you had better find out why.

"And these signs will follow those who believe: In my name they will cast out demons; they will speak with new tongues; they will take up serpents; and if they drink any- thing deadly it will by no means hurt them; they will lay hands on the sick, and they will recover," Mark 16:17-18.

If we were to take the bible literally, then I could honestly say, "If there are no signs in your church then there are no believers there either." Signs follow the believer. As this outpouring move closer, churches will begin to experience the signs and wonders. There are many more signs and wonders happening in the earth than those we are experiencing. I believe with this flood of supernatural power, signs and wonders will increase to the point where media can no longer hide them; they will in fact report them. Signs and wonders are meant for one purpose, to get the attention of the lost so you can bring the Word of God to them and get them saved.

"The sun shall be turned into darkness and the moon into blood before the day of the Lord," Acts 2:20.

Now that is an interesting portion of scripture. I wonder how God is going to accomplish that. I believe we may find some answers to my question in the Old Testament.

"And the Lord said to Moses, "Behold I come to you in the **thick cloud** that the people may hear when I speak with you, and believe you forever," Exodus 19:9a. "Now Mount Sinai was completely in **smoke** because the Lord descended upon it in **fire**. It's smoke ascended like the smoke of a furnace, and the whole mountain quaked greatly," Exodus 19:18.

"Now the **Glory of the Lord** rested on Mount Sinai, and the **cloud covered** it six days. And on the seventh day He called to Moses out of the **midst of the cloud**. The sight of the **Glory of the Lord** was like a **consuming fire** on the top of the mountain in the eyes of the children of Israel," Exodus 24:16-17.

"These words the Lord spoke to all your assembly, in the mountain from the **midst of the fire, the cloud, and the thick darkness**, with a loud voice; and he added no more. And He wrote them on two tablets of stone and gave them to me." So it was, when you heard the voice from the **midst of the darkness**, while the mountain was **burning with fire**, you came near me, all the heads of your tribes and your elders. And you said: "Surely the Lord our God has **shown us His Glory and His Greatness**, and we have heard His voice from the **midst of the fire**. We have seen this day that God speaks with man; yet he still lives," Deuteronomy 5:22-24.

"And I will show wonders in the heavens and in the earth: blood and **fire and pillars of smoke**," Joel 2:30.

The wonders we are about to experience are the manifestations of the Shekina Glory Cloud of God or His Manifested presence. I'm not talking about His omnipresence where He is everywhere at all times but His manifested presence where He shows up to pay a visit to your home, church, and community. God revealed His Glory to the children of Israel. He had to conceal Himself in thick darkness in order to prevent the children of Israel from being consumed. The bible says that the Lord is a fire from the loins up and a fire from the loins down. Sin cannot stand in the presence of the Glory of

God. He has to conceal Himself in thick clouds of darkness so as not to consume sinners when He manifests Himself.

All through the Old Testament we read where the Shekina Glory of God filled the temple. Where is God's temple today?

"Or do you not know that your body is the temple of the Holy Spirit who is in you, whom you have from God, and you are not your own?" 1 Corinthians 6:19.

The Shekina Glory of God will once again fill the temple. The Glory will fill the temple to overflowing. The bible says, "The whole earth shall be filled with the Glory of God," Psalm 72:19.

This spiritual flood is a flood of the Glory of God on this earth. The Glory will manifest to the degree of filling entire cities. The Shekina Glory Cloud will be so thick that sinners will not be able to see through it. They will be grouping around in it seeking help. The Apostle Paul experienced the Glory of God and it blinded him. After Paul was prayed for he could see again. You will have to pray for sinners to get born again in order for them to see through the cloud. The cloud will be so thick at day you will not see the sun, and at night the moon will appear blood red. The Holy Spirit is about to reveal Himself in His Fullness. Up to now we have had manifestations of His gifts or activities, but not His person to the measure that we are going to get.

WHOEVER SHALL CALL ON THE NAME OF THE LORD SHALL BE SAVED.

So (as the result of the Messiah's intervention) they shall (reverently) fear the name of the Lord from the west, and His Glory from the rising of the sun.
When the enemy shall come in like a flood, the Spirit of the Lord will lift up a standard

against him and put him to flight (for He will come like a rushing stream which the breath of the Lord drives)," Isaiah 59:19. I would like to call your attention to the comma after the word "Flood". Many people do not realize that the pronunciation marks, chapter, and verse were never in the original manuscripts. Bible scholars will tell you that pronunciation marks were inserted at the discretion of the translators. I believe the comma after the word flood is in the wrong place. It should be inserted after the word "in" instead of the word "flood". The phrase should read like this: "When the enemy comes in, like a flood the Spirit of the Lord will lift up a standard against him and put him to flight." That comma changes the power of the scripture!

    I have two reasons for believing the comma is misplaced:
1. The portion of scripture in brackets says, (For He [the Holy Spirit] will come like a rushing stream which the breath of the Lord

drives.) Now, you tell me if your street is flooded how can you drive the flood away with a garden hose? God is the rushing stream, which is flooding out the devil and sin.

"Having disarmed principalities and powers, He made a public spectacle of them, triumphing over them in it," Colossians 2:15.
A flood has power; Satan has none because Jesus disarmed him. By understanding the work of Calvary we see the magnitude of the victory Jesus attained for us. Jesus' triumph over Satan was so complete, stripping Satan of all authority and the keys of Hades and death that an open show, humiliating all satanic forces were made. Jesus made that spectacle of Satan to show us that he was defeated no matter what he tries to tell us to the contrary. Jesus tells us that the gates of hell would not prevail against the church.
Jesus also tells us that He has given us authority over all the power of the devil and

nothing shall harm us. To understand the New Covenant is to understand the position Christ attained for us. We are not trying to defeat an already defeated enemy. **WE ARE ENFORCING THE DEFEAT SATAN SUFFERED AT THE CROSS-BY THE BLOOD OF JESUS CHRIST, HIS DEATH AND RESURRECTION.** The enemy does not have the power or ability to come in like a flood against the church.

THE ENEMY CAN ONLY OPERATE TO THE DEGREE THE CHURCH ALLOWS HIM TO OPERATE.

History tells stories! At the Garden of Eden, Satan never came in like a flood. He had to trick, connive, and deceive his way into the affairs of man. It may seem like a flood of demonic activity in your neighborhoods and cities but it never started that way. I lived in Saskatoon Saskatchewan for a few years and came to find out that the city started as a religious colony; the standards of decency and morality were observed. After a while, very slowly, secular humanism and other Antichrist religions began to influence the people. The moral standards began to decline and the city sank deeper and deeper into idolatry and perversion and now we have present day Saskatoon. Saskatoon is typical of many cities and our country, starting out with pure motives, ending up on the scrap heap.

Our country has slowly sunk into decay and ruin. Some of our countries leaders give recognition to satanic churches and cults. Our people march for the right to save a seal or whale, yet in the same breath demand the right to murder their unborn children. This decay and ruin did not happen in one day. Satan introduced his ways, a little here a little there, slowly and well planned out. The church, being sung sweet songs and lullabies by devils has allowed Satan to come in virtually unchallenged.

The reason we think it is a flood is because we are finally awake and see how far we have sunk into moral decay and gross sin. But don't fear we are awake and are fighting back. When the enemy comes in, like a FLOOD the Spirit of the Lord (an ocean size flood) will lift up a standard against him and put him to **FLIGHT.** The church is a victorious church in every avenue of influence.

"Be glad then, you children of Zion, and rejoice in the Lord your God; for He has given you the former rain faithfully, and He will cause the rain to come down for you – the former rain and the latter rain in the first month," Joel 2:23.

"Let us know, let us pursue the knowledge of the Lord. His going forth is established as the morning; He will come to us like the rain, like the latter and the former rain to the earth," Hosea 6:3.

"Therefore be patient, brethren, until the coming of the Lord. See how the farmer waits for the precious fruit of the earth, waiting patiently for it until it receives the early and latter rain," James 5:7.

Hosea says the Lord will come like the rain, the former and the latter rain. Joel says the former and latter rain will be combined and come to us in a definite period of time. James says this rain will result in a harvest of the fruit (souls) of the earth.

The former rain represents the power and Glory of God manifested in the Old Testament. The latter rain represents the power and Glory of God manifested in the New Testament up to the present time. The power and glory of the old, along with the power and glory of the new, poured out upon us in one package. What a supernatural deluge. No wonder God showed me an ocean coming into shore in one wave. Are you ready for this event? Remember this event brings Jesus back for the church. Are you ready to stand confidently before the judgment seat of

Christ? Get ready church we are on the verge of Glory!!

ONCE UPON A TIME LONG, LONG AGO MY
SPIRIT BROKE FORTH TO SHOW THE MIGHTY
POWER OF THE LORD TO BRING JUDGMENT LIKE
A SWORD FROM THIS TIME I HAVE GONE
TO BRING FORTH GRACE WITH A SONG

THIS VERY DAY YOU SHALL SEE GLORIOUS
POWER WITH VICTORY
WHEN MY POWER STARTS TO FLOOD HONOR
MY PRESENCE THROUGH THE BLOOD

WHEN I COME THIS VERY NIGHT
RESURRECTIONPOWER GIVING SIGHT
GLORIOUS POWER YOU SHALL SEE COMING
FORTH TO VICTORY TO MY CHURCH I SHALL SAY

YOU HAVE ENTERED A SPECIAL DAY
BE BOLD, STRONG AND DILIGENT MY
RESURRECTION POWER I HAVE SENT
TO MY CHURCH I SHALL SAY
GET READY!! IT'S RESURRECTION DAY!

12 JOURNEY TO THE GLORY

This vision was given to me in March of 2002 at Victory Harvest fellowship in Camrose Alberta.
I see a group of people, walking individual paths through
A plush, green forest. Each path was designed for only one person. There were not couples or children together on the same path, only one person for one path. On each path there were pitfalls and obstacles and tests specifically designed for the individual.

    As the people emerged from the forest they emerged into an open meadow that led to the edge of a cliff. When the people arrived at the cliff they looked over and seen that it was a long way down. Looking at each other the people were not sure what to do next. Jesus was standing in the middle of the air facing the people. As they stood there looking Jesus began to talk "On the path you've come, this path is not to stray from. Closer and closer to the edge you are walking, keep coming hear me talking. I am drawing you to the place of freedom from your efforts. When you stand at the edge, faith will cause you to leap into my realm where there will be great comforts."

    Each Christian upon being born again starts a life long journey from the land of Egypt to Canaan, as did the Israelis people. In exodus 17 the children left the wilderness or desert of sin, where they experienced the sustaining power of God. No lack of food or clothes or other provisions were experienced while they journeyed through the wilder- ness; however they continued to test God.

The word journey in this context means "to

set aside", according to the Hebrew text. God has commissioned every born again Christian to have a journey or be set aside so that once the journey is completed they can experience the full- ness of his Glory. Our heavenly Father wants to pour out his Glory upon us without measure the same way he poured it out on Jesus.

Jesus spoke of this in John 17:22-24 "I have given these people the glory that you gave me so that they can be one, just as you and I are one. I will be in them and you will be in me so that they will be completely one. Then the world will know that you sent me and that you loved them just as much as you loved me. Father, I want these people that you gave me to be with me where I am. I want them to see my glory, which you gave to me because you loved me before the world was made."

    While we are on our journey through the forest we are going to experience many tests. Depending how far you are on your journey you can identify what I am talking about. These tests are not designed to destroy you (temptation is designed to destroy you). Tests are designed by God to show you what you really believe about God so you can correct the misbeliefs in your life.

James 1:1-16 bears this out, 1-8 "For James, a servant of God and of the Lord Jesus Christ. To all God's people who are scattered everywhere in the world: Greetings.
My brothers and sisters, when you have many kinds of troubles, you should be full of joy, because you know that these troubles test your faith, and this will give you patience. Let your patience show itself perfectly in what you do. Then you will be perfect and complete and will have everything you need. But if any of you needs wisdom, you should ask God for it. He is generous and enjoys giving to all people, so he will give you wisdom. But when you ask God, you must believe and

not doubt. Anyone who doubts is like a wave in the sea, blown up and down by the wind. Such doubters are thinking two different things at the same time, and they cannot decide about anything they do. They should not think they would receive anything from the Lord.

    12-16 when people are tempted and still continue strong, they should be happy. After they have proved their faith, God will reward them with life forever. God promises this to all who loves him. When people are tempted, they should not say, "God is tempting me." Evil cannot tempt God, and God himself does not tempt anyone. But people are tempted when their own desire leads them away and traps them. This desire leads to sin, and then the sin grows and brings death. My dear brothers and sisters do not be fooled about this. Every good action and every perfect gift is from God. These good gifts come down from the creator of the sun, moon, and stars, who does not change like their shifting shadows. God decided to give us life through the word of truth so we might be the most important of all the things he made.

Test in this text according to the Greek means to be accounted truthfully, be of reputation, examine, and discern, tried, and approved, acceptable, trustworthiness.

These are some of the tests you are going to have to go through.
1. How do you judge yourself? According to the flesh or according to how God sees and thinks about you.
2. If God loves you why can't you love you?
3. What do you believe about God?

How do you know when God is testing you? God is testing you when a situation arises and you have an emotional reaction other than peace. An emotional reaction other than peace is a trigger on the misbeliefs you have in your life.

Life on planet earth is about one thing and one thing only. What do you believe about God? Of course the Bible is our final authority on everything, so let's see what the Bible has to say about paths of life through the wilderness.

Psalms 16:11, you will show me the path of life; in your presence is fullness of joy; at your right hand are pleasures forevermore. Job 6:18, Travelers turn away from their paths and go into the desert and die. (The word desert in the Hebrew means wilderness and is interchangeable with desert. Both words mean the same thing.)

Job 19:8, God has blocked my way so I cannot pass; He has covered my paths with darkness. (Darkness here means to withhold the light, trials and tests.) Satan cannot stop the light of God's Word. Darkness flees when light is present. God is trying our hearts to show us what we really believe about him.

Psalms 23:3 He gives me new strength. He leads me on paths that are right for the good of His name.
(The Holy Spirit leads us, not your family members or your spouse.) If you do not develop an intimacy with the Holy Spirit yourself, you will stray from the path and go into the wilderness and die. No one can save you.
Psalms 17:5 uphold my steps in your paths that my footsteps may not slip.
Proverbs 2:8 He guards the paths of Justice and pre- serves the way of His saints.
Proverbs 12:28 In the way of righteousness are life and in its pathway there is no death.
The pathway of life that we are on is specifically designed by God for you individually to change from Glory to Glory to be changed into the image of Jesus. If you have received a Word from God concerning a situation in your life, whether

it came through the five-fold ministry or by the Holy Spirit and you haven't seen it manifest yet then check yourself and go develop an intimacy with the Holy Spirit and find the conditions that are required to see the Word from God fulfilled in your life.

All personal prophecies are conditional, example: You receive a Word from the Lord that He is going to bring in a lot of money to you and you receive it with excitement and start thinking about clearing up your debts and then thinking about how much you can give to the church, then your children, then what you can surround yourself with as far as creature comforts, and surely by Thursday or Friday you should see a major increase in salary or the lottery has favored you. You believe God and have a sense of joy for a few days. Then after a week nothing happens, a year and maybe two or three go by and you are still living the mundane life as before. Working two jobs paying bills, creating bills, barely surviving and always wanting more but never having enough no matter what effort you put into it. Finally you give up and except your lot in life and then criticize the person who gave you the message about money and determine in your heart that he or she is an imbecile and if they say anything to you again you will not listen because they produced a false hope in you and that isn't going to happen again.

    Don't feel bad or get into a condemning attitude I share your feelings. I have had the Holy Spirit speak to me directly in person so obvious that the only way you could not know who was speaking is if you were in hell where the Holy Spirit doesn't visit as far as I know. I have waited for over thirty years and now through a series of changes in my life am now in a position to see some of those things fulfilled in my life.

What I have learned about personal prophecies that come either from the Holy Spirit or from a member of the five-fold ministry is that they are markers on the path of life Jesus has put me on. The Holy Spirit reveals to others these markers to share with me to encourage me and strengthen me so I can continue walking the path of life and eventually reach the goal to be just like Jesus.

In the vision the edge of the cliff represents freedom from our own efforts. If you feel your efforts are still going to put you over the top and God is going to be impressed with what you accomplished for Him then I suggest you read Ecclesiastes 2 or maybe rather the whole book prayerfully taking stock of your life. When you are reading the last chapter of Ecclesiastes consider making Ecclesiastes 12:13 your priority in life. Jumping off the cliff and into the realm of God intrigued me so I asked God about it He gave me Ephesians chapter three. After a time of meditation, I finally perceived it. We are about to leap into the realm of God's love to the extent of fully understanding it. When we are there where we understand it and walk in it, manifesting God's love through us to a dying world then we will see the fullness of God poured out on us and through us. Jesus had the Holy Spirit without measure; we as His body are going to experience the same.

God's fullness on us and through us will cause the fulfillment of all personal prophecies that have been given from the heart of God. This fullness will also usher in the greatest harvest of lost souls into the kingdom of God in all the earths' history.

Are you ready to take a leap of faith into the realm of God's love? Have you strayed from the paths of life? Do you need prayer to help you find the path of life again?

13 ENCOURAGEMENT

I would encourage you to walk the repentant life. By living a repentant life free of sin and the cares of life, you can become a carrier of the Glory of the Lord. I would like to encourage you to walk in this higher life. It is available to anyone that will pay the price. Each person reading this writing will have different areas to deal with. By spending time in intercessory prayer the Holy Ghost can change, mold and purify your life. This is a book about repentance and preparation for the coming of Christ. Having a Holy walk before the Lord is needed by us and desired by the Lord.

    It seems people have a difficult time being free from sin. We excuse our behavior by saying, "everybody has sin and we all sin at some time." That excuse will no longer stand up! Lazy and undisciplined people try to justify them- selves. Freedom from sin starts in your heart. When in your heart you want to please God, more than anything else, you will begin to see bad habits and sin leave. A repentant heart, developed prayer life and a renewed mind to the Word of God, will keep you free from sin.

God needs you and can use you no matter who you are. God proved this to me twice. At one time people began to come down on me, condemning me and criticizing me because my life wasn't as pure and holy as they thought their lives were. I became very discouraged and frustrated because no matter how hard I tried I couldn't fulfill their high standards. People could not understand why the gifts of the Holy Spirit were being manifested in my life and not so much in theirs. I couldn't really tell you either at that time in my life. The only thing I could think of was that I gave my all to the Holy Spirit with reckless abandon. I grew up on the wrong side of life with no one but myself, so when I met Jesus I wasn't about to let go of Him for anything.

Even though people came against me I kept plugging away at what I knew to do. I tried to share my feelings with a certain pastor one time, sharing the areas that I felt God was using me in. I was never slapped down up to that time by someone's tongue like I was that day. The pastor looked me square in the eye and said in an ignorant voice, "Why would God use you when there is someone like me around!!" Talk about feeling rejected, the very man who was supposed to know God and encourage your growth, basically spat in your face.

Feeling totally rejected I was ready to quit; I knew I would never quit Jesus but it sure felt good to bellyache to God. I let God know exactly how I felt about these people. I was having my doubts about the gifts of the Holy Spirit and decided that maybe I shouldn't have God manifest them through me. God responded to my bellyaching quite sternly, **"WHO IS YOUR GOD ANYWAY, THEM OR ME**?" I said,

"You are." Then the Lord replied, **"THEN YOU GET IN THERE AND DO WHAT I TELL YOU TO DO."** I got the picture. My heart was right before God and as long as I walked in obedience to His Word, He would help me change my outer man. A pure repentant heart is what God is looking for. If you are of such a nature then God will use and develop you.

January 1993 reflecting back on the past eleven years of being in Christ I realized the changes in my life. From night to day, if you knew me in 1982 when I became a Christian and did a comparison you would say different people. Now in 2005 I look back and realize that I have changed so much, my nature and attitude are more in line with the Word of God. My lifestyle reflects Christ to a greater degree than it ever has, all because of a prayer I prayed in the fall of 1982. "Lord I am willing to be changed into the man that you want me to be, and in the areas that I am not willing, I am willing to be made willing."

Even though God has changed me drastically, He still is not finished with me. I hope to look back in a few more years and say to myself, "was I really like that man, God has changed me again." I look forward to change, reproof and correction. When God continually changes me to be more like Jesus I know He still loves me. While I can still be changed I look forward to change, so that one day I can look in the mirror and believe I am seeing a reflection of Jesus. No disrespect intended to my fellow man but I want to be that entire man God wants me to be not what man wants me to be. My outward appearance has changed over the years, areas that I used to say no way on this earth I would do that, I find myself doing. I used to be dead against piercing and tattoo's and now I have two piercing in my ear and a tattoo on my forearm. A fellow wandered into the church office one sunny afternoon and engaged me in conversation. Then for some reason he skillfully maneuvered me (or so he thought) to a passage of scripture dealing with the length of hair. Little did he know I had this chat about the length of a person's hair with many people? My hair at that time was shoulder length. After gently putting the scripture back into contents and letting him see it for what the bible really said I tried to explain to him that he had the wrong "H" word.

The length of your hair, the color of your skin or the size of your belly will not get you brownie points with God. Nor will it get you demerits in the kingdom of God. The attitude and condition of your heart is what God is interested in not the length of your hair. You know of course that if some physical attribute were the avenue to get blessings from God we would all be in serious trouble. For example if this fellow were right saying that God only likes people with short hair, I could get mine cut and be blessed but what about the bald man who has no hair in which to impress God? Church, it is time to put all this kind of silliness away. There are many people who have a heart for God but have been alienated from the church because their physical appearance is not to religious, Pharisaical standards. Sometimes I think someone should start a church called "The church of the physically freaky people who love Jesus with all their hearts." Stop looking to outward appearance and look to your heart to see if you are right before God.

The second time God proved He needed me was through a vision or some would call it a trance. I was reading a book called Lord Change Me during a slow day at work. Coming across a statement, which read, "God needs you," I thought this is the most pathetic statement I have ever read. After all, God doesn't need me because He has a lot of people He can use. Then my curiosity peaked and I asked the Lord, "You don't need me, do you?"
Instantly I went into a trance and a vision unfolded. Jesus was standing before me wearing the garments of a priest. We were standing beside a meadow with a creek running through it. Jesus bent down, picked

a pebble from the creek and said, "You are like this pebble. I will clean you, shine you, and perfect you. Then I will place you back into this creek bed; this creek would not be complete without you." Then very emphatically the Lord said, 'I need you!'" The vision ended, I was totally thrilled at what I had seen.

You are part of the Body of Christ. God needs you, your church needs you, and I need you. Without you, the body is incomplete. I need you and you need me. Together we can function and see God's plans fulfilled in the earth.

THE NAME

The name, which is above every name
Power and might found in the same
Love and compassion from whom does flow
This precious name we must know
At the sound of the name from above
Every knee shall bow, reaching for love

Of His Lordship they shall confess
Love of that name saints do express
To the exalted name from above
A heart of compassion filled with love

Who is this majestic mighty one?
Jesus Christ, the omnipotent Holy Son.

THE BIRTH OF A PSALMIST/PROPHET

14 PSALMIST

A psalmist of today would be one whose heart is after the heart of God. He would be one who delights to be in the presence of God and even longs to be. It would be his chief joy. He would be one who finds the time and the place to be alone with Him and has an intimate relationship with Him. He would find the time just to be quiet and still with Him and even basks in His presence.

He is like a painter with a blank canvas. The atmosphere is his canvas. He paints the mood in which the Holy Spirit is to move among His people. Sometimes his canvas takes on the mood of healing, sometimes gladness, and sadness, laughing in the spirit or whatever the need is. Sometimes his canvas takes on the mood of healing, sometimes gladness, and sadness, laughing in the spirit or whatever the need is. The psalmist has to be sensitive to what the Spirit is leading him to and flow in accordance. There is much mature fruit of the Spirit displayed in his life and also the gifts of the Holy Spirit. The Word of the Lord flows freely through him.

The psalms I would like to share are a reflection of God's heart to His people; A reflection of God's people to their creator. The psalms are a reflection of God's people to each other. I began writing psalms in 1988-1989 to the present. The first one was while I was attending my first year bible college. I was severely bored with the first year; it was like Sunday school classes when you were a preteen and you are twenty now. I was meditating on the Lord when I heard these words in my spirit.

RESURRECTION DAY

Once upon a time, long, long ago
My Spirit broke forth to show
The mighty power of the Lord
To bring judgment like a sword
From this time I have gone
To bring forth grace with a song

This very day you shall see
Glorious power with victory
When my power starts to flood
Honor my presence through the blood

When I come this very night
Resurrection power giving sight
Glorious power you shall see
Coming forth to victory

To my church I shall say
You have entered a special day
Be bold, strong and diligent
My resurrection power I have sent

To my church I shall say
Get ready! It's Resurrection Day!!

I wrote the words down quite calmly and after I read them I was excited. Something inside of me said the Holy Spirit has given me a new gift. Not sure what it was but I noticed the poem rhymed and it was prophetic in nature. I was later to learn this was the definition of a psalm. I showed my classmates and they were as intrigued as I. Later that day during another class something else started happening. I would glance at a classmate and an intense curiosity would rise up in me regarding them. I would hear words in my spirit and write them down. To my surprise they would ask how I knew the spiritual meaning to their name. I didn't I was just writing what I heard in my spirit. The students became excited and asked me to write a psalm for them. I just prayed because I knew I wasn't in charge but it was a prophetic gift of the Holy Spirit and it would only manifest as He wills. Over the years until 2017 I have wrote a few hundred psalms for people. I am sharing this psalm of an individual with her permission.

LAURIE

TO THE DAUGHTER OF FAITH
SAVED BY THE POWER OF GRACE
RESURRECTION STRENGTH STRONG AND TRUE
COMES UPON MY DAUGHTER TO DO

VICTORIES ARE COMING SO REJOICE
BLESSINGS ARE ABUNDANT, MAKE YOUR CHOICE
BOLDNESS AND CONFIDENCE TO YOU BELONG
RESURRECTION POWER IN A SONG

BOLDLY PROCLAIM MY RESURRECTED WORD
SIGNS AND WONDERS FOR THOSE WHO HEARD
MY GLORY SHALL BE REVEALED
MY WORD TO YOU IS A SHIELD

BE STRONG AND EXCITED, FILLED WITH LOVE
ON YOU IS MY SPIRIT FROM ABOVE
GO FORTH IN VICTORY DO NOT FEAR
RESURRECTION POWER TO THOSE WHO HEAR

I found this gift exciting as it took in many aspects of life. I found myself writing so regularly that I thought it was an endless supply. I want to jump ahead a few years to a time when the church I attended operated a booth called angels tent. This booth was at a county festival the town was having. The purpose of the booth was in response to a physic tent that read your palms and told your future according to Satan's will. The pastor brought in a facilitator who knew how to train people to move in the prophetic. You may say O' Come on. Let me tell you it is easier than you think.

Acts 2:17-21
King James Version
17 And it shall come to pass in the last days, said God; I will pour out of my Spirit upon all flesh: and your sons and your daughters shall prophesy, and your young

**men shall see visions, and your old men shall dream dreams:
18 And on my servants and on my handmaidens I will pour out in those days of my Spirit; and they shall prophesy:
19 And I will shew wonders in heaven above, and signs in the earth beneath; blood, and fire, and vapor of smoke:
20 The sun shall be turned into darkness, and the moon into blood, before that great and notable day of the Lord come: 21And it shall come to pass, that whosoever shall call on the name of the Lord shall be saved.**

The whole body of Christ has the ability to prophesy and move in the manifestations of the Holy Spirit. It's just unbelief that stops people from doing the works of God. People would come in and sit at one of the six tables we had in operation and receive a word from the Lord. If the facilitator at the table wasn't getting anything from the Holy Spirit they were trained to fall back on a scripture, **Jeremiah 29:11 for I know the plans I have for you," says the LORD. "They are plans for good and not for disaster, to give you a future and a hope.**

    I would write poems for people and they would go away excited and happy that the God of heaven would take time to communicate with them. Religion has taught us that the God of heaven is not interested in communicating with us. However the opposite is true. God desires fellowship with His people.
2 Corinthians 13:14. May the grace of the Lord Jesus Christ, and the love of God, and the fellowship of the Holy Spirit be with you all.
    Over a two day period we had one-hundred and fifty new decisions for Jesus and seventy-five recommitments. I took a break and went for a walk and noticed the Spirit of God dealing with individuals in the crowd. When I got back to the angel tent the Spirit of God instructed me to go in the

back to the intercession prayer area and pray. As I prayed the Spirit of the Lord gave me four poems with the instructions to give them the facilitators at the table. If the facilitator got nothing then they were to give the Individual a poem. One poem was about the Spirit of God sitting down with a musician and writing songs together. You guessed it; an individual who was a musician sat down and got that poem. He went away quite excited.

Another poem was about having a second chance. Earlier a couple of sisters sat at a table and received a word from the Lord and one of them accepted Jesus. The other said no. it was getting on into the evening so the one sister decided it was time to go home and cook dinner for her family. The other sister decided to come back to the angel tent and see if maybe God had something privately for her. The facilitator at her table was getting nothing, and then she remembered the poem. She handed the woman the poem explaining how someone in the back who never seen her wrote it specifically for her. The woman read it then broke down and cried telling her story. She was here earlier but decided not to accept Jesus. The poem spoke directly to that situation encouraging her of God's great love for her. She accepted Jesus and went away a new creation. Back to the bible college, where this gift was in its infancy and being enjoyed by all. After a few days of writing for people I got a poem dealing with wives.

A GODLY WIFE

Virtuous and compassionate full of love
She is God's gift sent from above
To this woman I shall impart
Wisdom and knowledge to fill her heart
The fear of the Lord makes her just
In her, her husband does trust
To this woman I shall say
Receive my anointing this very day
I shall guide you through your life
Receive my anointing dear Godly wife
Integrity and honor are yours to stay
You shall be blessed day by day.

I read this poem to the class and right away they wanted one about a Godly husband. I told them I would pray about it and I did and within an hour I received this poem.

A GODLY HUSBAND

Prophet, Priest and a King
The Word of God he does bring
Protects and serves from a pure heart
Being a provider is but a start
He is the image and glory of the Lord
Fearlessly wielding the two edged sword
A strong, bold and powerful life
He'll gladly lay it down for his wife
Love and compassion from who does flow
To him his wife will gladly go
A strong bridge over the pressures of life
He'll be blessed with a godly wife

I was surprised when one woman said that wasn't quite what she was looking for. I told her to go to God and get one for herself. I just write what I hear in my spirt and it isn't up to me if people like them or not. As time continued I would get inspiration from many different sources. I knew I was writing about a person when the curiosity factor rose. Most of the psalms I write seem to flow in a rhyming factor but I soon found out that this would not be a pattern set in stone. Here is an example.

I SEE A HOT AIR BALLOON FLYING HIGH ABOVE THE CLOUDS. DEAN AND VI ARE IN THE BASKET. ROPES ARE HANGING FROM THE BASKET. PEOPLE ARE REACHING FOR AND GRABBING THE ROPES. WHEN THEY GRASP THE ROPES, THE ROPES ALONG WITH THE PEOPLE MUST BE TRANSPORTED HIGHER THAN THE BALLOON, THUS MAKING THE HOT AIR BALLOON A LAUNCHING OFF PLACE. AS HOT AIR SENDS A NATURAL BALLOON HIGHER SO SHALL THE WIND OF MY SPIRIT LAUNCH AND CARRY YOUR BALLOON HIGHER AND GUIDE IT'S DIRECTION TO PLACES AND HEIGHTS ONLY DREAMED OF. ARE YOU READY TO LIFT OTHERS HIGHER THAN WHAT YOU PERCEIVE YOU ARE?

Bible College was a unique experience where the anointing of a psalmist began but never gave me a direction for my life. It just left me with a large student loan to pay back. I am not against Bible College and if you sense the Holy Spirit telling you to go then you should have gone already. I went because of pressure from pastors and other spiritual leaders. Funny thing was they never mentioned that I might think about the school across the river. I was to attend their school which was a part of their church. Enough rambling, after completing the two year course I left and found the psalmist anointing increased. There is only so much you can do in the four walls of the church or religious setting. The real ministry starts where people live their lives every day not just three hours a week. I wish I could find the song from the eighties that was my favorite. Some of the lyrics were, "some people want a position within the churches four walls but I want a ministry a yard from the gates of hell." If someone reading this knows the song and how I can get it please let me know. I am on Facebook like most of the North American population. I love this anointing because there is no rhyme or reason on how it kicks in. I am driving down the highway and my attention was drawn to a tree sitting in the middle of a field by itself. This is the psalm that came from that situation.

HOME

Alone and majestic it does stand
Strong arms reaching out so grand
Bringing protection to those below
An umbrella from the deep snow
Standing upright in an open field
To others its fruit to yield
What is this sight I see?
But a lonely spruce tree
Many look and see no good
Just a big old chunk of wood
But to the animals which do roam
This tree is called home
There is a moral to this psalm
Don't condemn just be calm
Others may not measure up
But who's to say what's their cup

This psalm so reminded me of a church I attended. During the eighties my first wife and I had a ministry among street people. We won bikers, prostitutes and witches to Jesus. We would bring them to church hoping to incorporate them into the fold. Problem was they didn't look like the rest of the suits and ties and were looked down on. Realizing this we started a bible study with them and it began to grow. We were sitting with over thirty with children when it caught the attention of the church leaders. I attended this church on a regular basis because I was part of its bible college. I was called in and told that I couldn't have a bible study. I explained the situation about bringing them but they were being looked down by other members of the congregation. As soon as I told them that these street people were gladly donating large sums of money to the church the attitude changed. I was told I could have a bible study but the people could only come for a month then I would have to send them away. I could not do that because it takes more than a month to make newly born again sinners into saints.

    Discipleship takes time and you can't force it. Nevertheless I had a choice to make, the religious institution or people. I chose people and left the church. Some of the people wanted us to start a church but sad to say that adventure wasn't in the cards. I was really disappointed when friends of mine who still attended the church told me the pastor was preaching against me. He was telling the congregation not to attend any bible study or meeting I might have because I had a demonic influence over people.

    How are we going to win the lost to Jesus with this sort of pettiness in the church? Be careful on how you judge.

Matthew 7:1-3King James Version (KJV)
7 Judge not, that ye be not judged.
2 For with what judgment ye judge, ye shall be judged: and with what measure ye mete, it shall be measured to you again.
3 And why beholdest thou the mote that is in thy brother's eye, but considerest not the beam that is in thine own eye?

We eventually found places for the people to fellowship in before we left Saskatoon. I heard a few years later that some of the natives that attended our study started their own church. It wasn't long after the pastor preached against me that some of the under handed activities of the leadership came to light. Money raised for projects seemed to vanish and the pastor built himself a new house in a gated community and a cabin by the lake. The church is but a shell of what it used to be. I am not saying that stuff happened because of the pastor coming against me. I am saying if God is moving in a direction you are not familiar with please don't make judgments because they will come back to bite you. I believe we are living in Revelation 2-3 where God is judging the church to prepare it for the resurrection. God desires us to be humble and not judge by what we see in the natural.

Done Bible College with this great word of encouragement from the dean, "don't be discouraged if you don't get into any kind of ministry you dreamed about because eighty percent of bible college graduates never enter into ministry." Thanks a lot why did you pressure me to attend your college for two years if there is no ministry future for me afterwards. Oh well I guess that was the course of life. So you go find a job and continue to support your family but now a large student loan to pay off as well.

So you do what every person does. You talk with God about it and rest knowing god has everything in control. I heard many sermons on waiting on the Lord. Problem was I am not the waiting type, if I think it I try to do it immediately. The Lord gave me some encouragement with the following psalms.

WAIT UPON THE LORD

Those who wait upon the Lord
Shall be tempered as a two edged sword
They shall walk and not tire
The anointing of God lifts them higher

They shall run and not pass out
In victory songs they do shout
Honor and integrity are their lot
The grace of God they have sought

They shall mount up with wings as an eagle
Splendorous they soar, O so regal
They shall walk in robes of royal thread
Blessed be the Word I have read.

I guess just trust the Lord and put my hand to the plow and don't look back. One thing I did know after experiencing the ministry team and pastor of that church organization I was turned off on being a pastor, I even commented on that to the head pastor. I guess being a young Christian with no diplomacy developed in my life I never knew not to burn bridges, I just blew them up. I guess you would expect that from a carnal Christian with more zeal than wisdom.

The thing I rejoiced in was that God knew my heart even if my head was in la la land. My heart was after God and I just needed to grow more in the spirit. The Lord gave me the following psalm to encourage me.

A SPIRITUAL MAN

A spiritual man upright and true
Integrity and love thru and thru
Spiritual pride is not his lot
The grace of God he has sought
A spiritual man quite contagious
Against him the enemy rages
Victories are known through the land
In the power of God he must stand
A spiritual man faithful and true
With him no days are blue
A priest and king he shall be
When Jesus comes for you and me.

After Bible College everything seemed to fall apart. No job and Christmas was around the corner so you do what you know to do and that is talk with God. Not like most prayer meetings I have experienced where people have a list of request that they talk at God about but never wait around to hear His response. The Lord gave me this psalm to encourage me.

FAITHFULNESS

I will exalt my only hope
Through your Word I can cope
When life is futile, full of disaster
I shall jump, shout, be filled with laughter
When my world comes crashing down
I'll sing and dance with no frown
Because of kindness, grace, and love
I shall praise you who is above
A new day is dawning I shall see
Your Word will guide through eternity
In song and dance I have praised
On that third day you were raised
Praise and thanks I stand strong
Because to whom I do belong
You are my hope, mighty king
I will praise you in everything.

Christmas was coming and we were invited to go to Grande Prairie and spend it with my cousin. We got in our little chevette and headed down the highway, only to have the engine blow in minus forty weather. I pulled over to the side of the road put on my four way flashers, lifted the hood of my car and the steam and oil poured out. Thank God he knew ahead of time my situation and had a trucker a couple of miles behind me. This sixteen wheeler semi pulled over and we loaded our luggage into his rig along with my wife and our two small children. He drove us to Edmonton where we met up with my sister and borrowed their little truck to go the rest of the way to Grande Prairie for Christmas vacation. I rejoiced because our helper the Holy Spirit saved us from a potential life threatening situation.

FEAR NOT

Fear not, fear not, and fear not
I am the salvation you have sought
To deliver you by the power of my blood
The enemy may roar but he's no flood
Through the power of my name
To you salvation has already came

Fear not, fear not, and fear not!
My blood your salvation has bought
Fear not! Look to the king on high
Let your praises ascend to the sky
Resurrection power on the way
To deliver from harm every day.

HELPER

The helper is one to whom you must run
When battles are to be won
Imparting bravery, strength and might
Be valiant, be brave, and continue to fight
When in weakness, lost or confused
Resist the enemy, don't be abused
The helper is there to lend a hand
In the power of God you shall stand
Who is this helper? What's His name?
The Holy Spirit, the one and the same
The enemy comes, bringing strife
Run to the author of all life
He is your help in time of need
Of His instruction do take heed
Author of life to one and all
Bless God! I'm redeemed from the fall.

Christmas came and went and with the help of my sister and brother in law we moved to Edmonton Alberta to start a new life. I was glad that God brought people into our lives to encourage us because life was looking pretty bleak at this time.

THE ENCOURAGER

Who is this one who brings encouragement?
Obviously one whom heaven has sent
She reaches out when others are down
Imparting hope and smiles
In the place of a frown

Who is this one from whom strength flows
On her my anointing continually grows
Bringing joy and peace to all her peers
She reaches out to wipe their tears

To this child I shall say,
My peace on you shall continually stay
To the one who looks to others best?
Enter thou into my Holy rest.

I took a job as a maintenance man at an apartment complex. After about six months I moved back to Grande Prairie where I am living today. Ordained in 1998 and served as an associate pastor for a few years. I did the work of the ministry that was set before me. I resumed my job as a roofer to provide for my family. Ministry seemed lost and going nowhere so I just relaxed and worked as a roofer. The psalms started coming randomly with no pattern at all. The subjects varied. One particular day when life seemed discouraging and the wife was looking at you like you were just a dreamer and nothing of reality would be produced in your life; the Lord gave me this psalm.

HUSBAND TO HIS WIFE

To the one who's a gift from above
You are beautiful in whom I find love
Please be patient with me every day
I sometimes get confused and lose my way
Don't be angry or full of strife
I too am filled with resurrection life
Please be an encourager when my days are blue
Because truly, I do love you
I am being changed; God's tugging at my heart
Life's a challenge; I want to do my part
Hold me tight, I need your love
Cut me slack, don't push or shove

I am a man who's sensitive at heart
But my feelings I don't easily impart
Soon I will rise up in the right hour
Flowing with God's resurrection power.

When you are doing a job that becomes routine and you can think you can do it in your sleep; you pray in the spirit while you work. This is some of the fruit of praying in tongues while you worked. I had to keep a notepad and pen handy because I never knew when I was going to get a psalm. I remembered a dream I had when I was just a few months old as a Christian and this psalm explains it exactly.

THE BLOOD

Standing on the edge of the universe
Proclaiming the Word, but not in verse
Standing tall and strong
Proclaiming words that weren't wrong
Bold and confident I have said
His precious blood has been shed
There I stand where all could see
Proclaiming the blood for eternity
Of His blood I do not plead
Boldness and confidence is what I read
Proclamation of that great name
The powerful blood I will
PROCLAIM!!!!

One Sunday I was asked to preach. I brought the children up for prayer and prayed and dismiss them to their classes. Watching the children put the seed for a psalm in my heart.

CHILDREN

**Wide eyed and innocent of all wrong
Sit the children of this psalm
Confident, trusting, willing to share
The love they experience there**

**Through these doors my children come
To learn the integrity of my Son
The teachers have quite the task
To answer questions the pupils ask**

**Love, kindness and righteousness they yearn
Please help my children to learn
Teachers walk upright, do your part
To give the children a righteous start.**

After church services you usually go for lunch with friends. Every now and then you end up with a large group of people. The following psalm was written at the table while the group was eating and fellowshipping.

COMPANIONS

When we are among friends
The anointing He does send
To keep our thoughts on high
For our praises to ascend to the sky

We are a cheerful joyous lot
The grace of God we have sought
Let us encourage and strengthen each other
There's a friend who sticks closer than a brother

Red, white, yellow and blue
Will we be friends quite true?
Looking to the others best
Let's pursue the Word with zest.

As I began to grow in the anointing of a psalmist I found myself writing psalms for people who were going through negative situations in life. People need love expressed from God to them continually because this world pulls them down. This psalm I wrote to one of God's daughters. No name was mentioned so it can be piggy backed by every daughter of God who needs encouragement.

DAUGHTER OF THE LORD

To this young child I shall say
Rejoice, rejoice, coming is a better day
Strength and honor I shall impart
To my daughter of a gentle heart

My love extends with resurrection life
Walk in love not in strife
To my daughter I shall say
Search my heart, continue to pray

To the daughter of my grace
I behold your lovely face
I rejoice because your mine
To you my love will forever shine.

Sorry if it seems like I am bouncing from subject to subject but that is how the psalms started coming. No rhyme or reason just random. This next psalm came because of the end times we are living in and Satan is raging in fury across the planet.

DEVIL'S DEMISE

The anointing is flowing
The gifts are growing
The devil is in fear
Because his end is near

When the devil roars in strife
Know for sure he's at the end of his life
Though he connives and does try
Know for sure his attempts will die

Victory is yours for sure
Because of a heart that's pure
Jesus Christ the King on high
Has destroyed the enemy, it's time for him to die

We are in a spiritual war and when you walk in holiness you can say what Jesus said in john 14:30 New International Version I will not say much more to you, for the prince of this world is coming. He has no hold over me. It is easier to do warfare when we are walking upright before god then the devil can't bring railing accusations against us and we have victory over his attacks. We go through battles and experience victories again and again. It seems to be endless and we just want to give up but we know there is one to who we can look.

GOD OF COMFORT

My Savior and hope of whom I'll sing
Guides and comforts in everything
To my soul he does impart
His mighty peace to settle my heart
When the entire world roars with strife
His great love brings me life
From the cross come blessings more
The chastisement for our peace He has bore
When confusion turns my head
Of His Word I have read
Quiet and confidence is my part
Peace and comfort does fill my heart.
Our focus has to be on Jesus because
He is the only one that can give us a life
Worth living.

GOD IN THE HIGHEST

Praise be to God from whom all blessings
Flow
With love and worship, to Him I shall go
He is my fortress and strong tower
My Jesus comes with resurrection
power

He is the light and joy of life
Keeping me from harm and all strife
He is my soon coming King
Bringing joy and causing all to sing

He is the one who looks to my best
Giving joy, peace and eternal rest
Of all the things that come my way
I'll look forward to resurrection day.

When others demean you and act like
You have no value remember there is
Someone who values you beyond
measure.

GOD'S BEST

You are worth more than you know
Study my Word, continue to grow
Be strong, you're a child of the king
Success and honor in everything

Your destiny brings ultimate success
Don't say no, just say yes
Full of life you shall be
When in faith you look to me

Excitement and power, the fruit of life
Wisdom and honor, the absence of strife
Grace and wonders, child of the King
You are blessed in everything.

No matter what a person goes through we have an anchor.

THE WORD

The Word is precious to me
Upholding and strengthening for eternity
The Word brings healing this I know
In times of trouble to the Word I go

Powerful, living, sharp and quick
The Word delivers those that are sick
In the Word I find sustenance
Guiding and directing to repentance

I'm in love with the righteous Word
Inspiring faith in all who heard
The Father, the Word, the Holy One
Set free to worship the righteous Son.

With all the activity in my life one thing stands out. The desire I had when I talked with Jesus when I was ten. To be a preacher, not necessarily a pastor but a preacher.

PREACHER

To be a preacher of the Word
Blessing the many who have heard
To skillfully wield the two edged sword
Being a vessel of the Lord

Son of man hear my Word
Bless the many who have heard
Store my sayings in your heart
Deliver My Word that's your part

Son of man, this I say
Study the Word every day
Go to the people, tell them so
Whether they say yes, whether they say No

Blessed is the Lord from His place
Being a preacher is only through grace
I'll skillfully preach the mighty Word
Blessing the many who have heard.

The more I study God's word the more I realize I need a deeper revelation of God's grace.

GRACE

Amazing grace how sweet the sounds
Because of love that knows no bounds
I was lost in sin and undone
Redeemed through the cross of your only Son

Grace came with blessings by the score
Jesus stands knocking at our heart's door
Will I let the righteous one in?
To save and redeem from the power of Sin

Hosanna in the highest, Holy, Holy one
I receive you in my heart, Jesus the Son
Because of grace you were raised
Forever now to be praised.

As my journey in life continues I find one place I desire to be above all else and that is in His presence.

THE PRESENCE

With pureness of heart I shall stand
In your presence O so grand
Majestic angels all around
Rejoicing! A glorious sound

I shall stand before you on that day
Until then I will continue to pray
Your presence, I have sought
With your blood I was bought

I am a child of the most high
In your presence, my tears you shall dry
In your presence I shall stand
Rejoicing in song O so grand.

I found the fastest way into the presence of God is to honor the blood of Christ.

THE BLOOD

**Standing on the edge of the universe
Proclaiming the Word, but not in verse
Standing tall and strong
Proclaiming words that weren't wrong**

**Bold and confident I have said
His precious blood has been shed
There I stand where all could see
Proclaiming the blood for eternity**

**Of His blood I do not plead
Boldness and confidence is what I read
Proclamation of that great name
The powerful blood I will PROCLAIM!!!!**

Earlier I mentioned the angel's tent. One thing I forgot to mention was the reason

I left the tent and went for a walk. I started to experience an open heaven.
When the heavens are open revelation flows so freely it almost is too much for the soul to handle.

OPEN HEAVENS

Open heavens are the things you want
Closed heavens are the devil's taunts
When you release those rivers of water
The devil shall flee because of his slaughter

When in intercessory prayer you fight
Beams and shafts of Holy light
Shall penetrate the blanket of dark
Be fervent because there is a great spark

Be strong, faithful and ready to fight
Because you shall see darkness blasted by light
Faith and confident you shall stand
Glorious victory o so grand!

When you are operating under an open heaven winning souls to Jesus becomes much easier.

SOULWINNER

**Wise, wise, wise is this man you see
Helping others to change their destiny
He is the one who heeds my instruction
Saving others from their own destruction**

**His love for life you shall know
When reaching to others the anointing Flows
To this one full of life
Integrity and honor with no strife**

**This is a man who knows my ways
Spending time with me, ordering his Days
This is a child of the most high
Reaching out until the day he dies.**

To be affective at winning people to Jesus you first have to be an effective prayer warrior.

WARRIOR

A warrior is one who stands to fight
For everything he believes is right
Sin and unrighteousness he will not
Condone

He will continue to stand, even if alone
The weapons of his warfare he does
Know
The battle cry has sounded; he is the first
To go

Wise and cunning he proceeds to fight
For everything he believes to be right
This one is special don't you see
Helping others to attain liberty

Humble and honorable, quite so real
Resurrection power when he kneels
When a battle rages here or there
He shall proceed through Word and
Prayer
The Lord is raising an army you see
To March to war; on their knees.

I am glad that Jesus chose me to be a psalmist because the revelation I get and the spiritual growth I develop causes joy in my heart. Sometimes I get a picture from God's point of view like the following psalm declares.

MESSIAH

My God! My God! Why do you forsake me?
Great is the suffering, don't you see?
I am the one who paid for sin
Lift your head, stand and grin

I paid the price for all you've done
You are delivered from the evil one
I was raised by great power
It will soon be resurrection hour

Your righteousness is of me
My blood has set you free
I am the Messiah who suffered for you
Accept my love, for it is true

I am exalted, lifted on high
Rejoice, rejoice, and do not cry
I am the Lord who set you free
Forever mine, you shall be.

The messiah has a name and his name is JESUS.

JESUS

Jesus Christ, the Lord my rock
In His presence I shall walk
Glory and strength, full of love
My dear Jesus, sent from above

Strength and honor He will impart
To everyone who is pure of heart
Kindness radiates from His eyes
A man of integrity, with no lies

The Lord my Savior, full of grace
Gentleness shines from His face
Love extends and knows no bound
A greater God, who has found?

It took me awhile but eventually I got the revelation that Jesus paid for our sickness the same time and place, the cross, that he paid for sin.

HEALING

I was bruised for your iniquities
Look to me not your remedies
I am the Lord of all your health
Healing breaks forth in overflowing Wealth

I am the healer, great is my supply
Look to me, you shall not die
I was wounded for your transgressions
Your healing comes in many successions

By my stripes you have been healed
With my Spirit you were sealed
Use my name, be so quick
I've delivered you, don't be sick.

The bible says Jesus name is above every name.

THE NAME

**The name which is above every name
Power and might found in the same
Love and compassion from who does
Flow
This precious name we must know**

**At the sound of the name from above
Every knee shall bow, reaching for love
Of His Lordship they shall confess
Love of that name saints do express**

**To the exalted name from above
A heart of compassion filled with love
Who is this majestic mighty one?
Jesus Christ, the omnipotent Holy Son.**

His name is so high even nature worships Him.

NATURE

The birds, flowers and trees do sing
Rejoicing in the Lord their melodies ring
Watching the sun about half past five
When all of a sudden the breeze was Alive

As the breeze continued on bye
The name of Jesus was exalted on high
As the anointing began to flow
A new revelation for me to know

Then one day while reading the Word
All excited over the phrase I heard
Sun, moon and stars of light
Praise His name this very night.

Many Christians fall short of the life Christ has for us. We were never meant to live on barely get by avenue and the corner of lacking street. We were made in the image of God and should be living as overcomers.

VICTORY

The Lord my King, the heavenly rock
Of your exploits I shall talk
You are the one who set me free
Anointed my life for total victory

You have made me more than a conqueror
I'm not beaten, trodden under, or sore
Your divine power has given to us all
Redemption and victory from the fall

When terror comes by night
I'll stand in confidence not in fright
Pestilence comes, I'll not fear
Rejoice in the Word that I hear

You are the one who set me free
Anointed my life for total victory
Living stones to me you talk
I'm a chip off the heavenly rock.

Not only is Jesus my messiah and savior He is also my shepherd who guides me and watches over me.

THE SHEPHERD

O my King! To you I'll sing
You have blessed in everything
All around, the shadow of death
I'm delivered by your breath

The breath of life fills my heart
On the paths of righteousness I shall start
Of the evil I will not fear
Because of your presence O so near

Power and authority I do know
My enemy runs, watch him go
Boldness and mercy all of my life
Quiet times with no strife

I'll live in the house of the Lord
Protected by your two edged sword
Your testimony and covenant I shall keep
Because your anointing guides my feet.

Prosperity and healing preachers are declared as the other gospel which is apparently not of God. I think these people should think twice about judging the Word of God. I think God gives clues to His ideas on success in the following psalms.

SUCCESS

You are my rock and fortress
The Lord of all my success
Spirit, soul, and body, you want my best
Your Word, I'll pursue with zest

When pressure tries my faith
I'll walk in the Word of Grace
You will never leave me in a spot
I'll not allow my harvest to rot

I am the Lord of all your success
In righteous ways you shall dress
Honor, integrity and pureness of heart
Covenant power for a successful start.

To be a true success you have to know God's heart.

THE GIVER

The giver is one who knows my heart
Giving of themselves is a righteous start
Fulfilling the conditions they have heard
Reaping the promises of My Word

The rut of poverty they shall not see
Their giving will excel throughout Eternity
Of My ways they have heard
Reaping the promises of My Word

The giver is somebody who touches my Heart
Tithes and offerings is only a start
The love of God they have heard
Reaping the promises of My Word.

My journey in life never really consisted of anybody I could call father or dad. I had a step-father that tried to do right to the best of his abilities. Unfortunate thing for him was he was suddenly a step father to someone else's children at the ripe old age of forty-five. He tried his best and I will give him that.

But one thing that was consistent in my life was my mother. My mother is in heaven now enjoying the presence of Jesus and my step-father who gave his life to Jesus just before he died. Mom this psalm is for you.

MOTHER

Patient and gentle she does stand
Kindness and grace are hers to command
Peace and contentment with no strife
She lives a quiet and Godly life

In wisdom and knowledge she does Grow
With gentle words she helps us to know
The guidance to fulfill our lives part
Love comes from the depths of her heart

Power and strength to radiate
Disobedience she does hate
A gift of heaven she is from
I'll look forward to calling her... MOM.

In this day and age trouble abounds and hearts are hard. What can be said about you?

TEARS ON A SHOULDER

The tears on your shoulder are there for a reason
The person who left them there was expressing emotion
Joy or sorrow, who can say,
What the emotion of the day

The real question I have to ask
The shoulder cried on is it a task
Many will be bothered by the tear
The color on my sweater is smeared

Are you full of love fulfilling your part?
Your shoulder, a place for others to lay their heart
Satisfaction will be yours I can say
When on your shoulder hearts can lay

We are living in the closing period of the end times with the soon return of Jesus.

THE RIDER

In the clouds O so high
Comes a rider from the sky
On a powerful steed standing true
A resurrected King comes to you

The Word of God is His name
A two edged sword proceeds from the same
Behold the greatness of His power
To bring judgment in that hour

All you who stand to mock
Prepare to be crushed by the Rock
To you who rejoice at His command
Resurrection life will cause you to stand

The book of revelation talks about two suppers. My question to you friend is what supper are you going to attend?

THE SUPPER OF THE LAMB

A banqueting table, the supper of the Lord
A place of honor or judgment with the sword
Blessing and glory and honor and power
Or judgment in that final hour

Blessings at the marriage supper of the Lamb
A place of honor for the worshippers of the "I Am"
The birds that fly in the midst of heaven
Dine on meat with no leaven

Rejoice, the marriage of the Lamb
Servants arrayed in the linen of the "I Am"
Out of His mouth goes a sharp sword
To strike the ungodly horde

The supper of the Lamb! Let us rejoice
A great choir all of one voice
Hide us from the wrath of the Lamb
We are enemies of the "I Am"

The question is to you my friends
Which stanza to you to send
A child of the great "I Am"
Or an enemy of the Lamb?

My desire when it is all said and done is to stand in the throne room of my Father God and join in with the countless angels and saints to give praise and worship to the most
high. I enjoy and even crave for His presence and one day it will be permanent.

THRONEROOM

A voice majestically does sound
Thunder and lightning's all around
Twenty four elders clothed in white
Seven lamps burning bright

The living creatures O what a sight
Crying Holy, Holy day and night
Thousands of angels all around
All together with one sound

Worthy, worthy is the Lamb
Power and Honor to the I am
Blessing and honor, glory and power
To the Lamb in that grand hour

We are all on a journey through this life. Many people look for the destination and are so focused on it they don't enjoy the journey. People at times ask how your day is. This question does not get answered truthfully, because if it was answered truthfully most not all would answer according to their emotional state at the moment. Through my life and the anointing (teaching) not to answer most questions emotionally. I am on a journey and I have adventures every day. If I go to sleep in peace then I have conquered the day with its adventure. If I am not in peace then the day is not done until I put my head on my pillow with peace flowing through my heart and soul.

JOURNEY TO THE DESTINATION

Many look and see the destination
They run but only to be disappointed
They fail to realize the organization
Of what they see is time appointed

The journey they fail to see
Is what prepares them for eternity?
The journey the great adventures and joy
Is troubling but trust me emotions not a
Toy

The journey builds character and
strength
The destination takes away my breath
The joy the journey those received
The destination a supernatural rift

This has been my journey as a psalmist for approximately thirty years. It is by no means over. It seems that a person goes through dry spells then a spiritual flood of activity. In the
following sections I will continue to share

my journey. Not as a psalmist but as a member of the five-fold ministry. I pray the psalms written here will be a source of encouragement to you and even revelation to how much God cares and desires your ultimate success.

15 THE CALL

Unknown to me the Holy Spirit was planning a supernatural visitation as soon as the household had retired for the night. Well into the early hours of the morning a light illuminating the interior of our house awakened me. Something
was drawing me to the source of the light. As I walked into the kitchen I realized the light started outside radiating in. I was compelled into the porch and outside to the steps. The most
marvelous sight I had ever seen appeared in the sky above me. A large pair of hands appeared in the sky held together
in prayer. The hands began to open and a

bible appeared. This bible was so huge it seemed to fill the entire sky. I stood in awe as a passage of scripture was circled.

The scripture was Ezekiel 3:10-11, "Moreover He said to me: "Son of man, receive into your heart all my words that I speak to you, and hear with your ears. And go, get to the captives, to the children of your people, and
speak to them and tell them, 'Thus says the Lord God,'
whether they hear, or whether they refuse."

After a minute or so of watching this scene I was translated to the far end of my stepfather's grain field. My brothers and sisters were with me. We were standing beside the flat top hay wagon when Jesus appeared. He was wearing
royal purple robes and radiated the most brilliant light I had ever seen. The glory radiating from Christ was so brilliant that creation ceased to exist, all you could see was Jesus and His glory, and nothing else

was visible.

Jesus stood before us, His hand extended to us. In His hand was a piece of fruit of some sort. He presented this fruit to us, we all stood staring not sure what to do. I took the fruit from His hand and stood in amazement looking at this fruit, as it was not like anything we had ever seen. I decided to take a bite of the fruit. As soon as I bit off a piece of the fruit, the vision ended, I was sitting on the edge of my bed, daylight pouring in through the windows, wondering about the events that just took place.

I never really understood that vision as a child, but one thing was very clear to me; from that time on I wanted to be a minister of the Gospel of Jesus Christ. Life continued on for a young child, school during the week, work on the farm and Sunday school during the weekends. This lifestyle continued until I was fifteen and puberty set in and I experienced a new revelation. Girls now becoming young women, they were no longer funny looking boys to throw mud at and make fun of, but someone you wanted to impress in the worst way.

I moved out of home and to my uncle's house as my family was falling apart. My mother and step father were having marriage problems and would eventually divorce.
I spent the next few years travelling around British Columbia,
Alberta and Saskatchewan. I found a beautiful woman and married her and had a son. We were in the process of settling down to a quiet life and raising children. Christianity and religion was not part of our life even though my wife had mentioned that she used to go to Sunday school when she was a little girl.

We had what we thought was a normal Canadian lifestyle, full time job with a pay cheque every two weeks, then a time of relaxation partying with friends. My cousin Victor showed up one evening while we had a small party going on and he asked my wife and me if we would baby sit his son while him and his wife went out for a time of relaxation. We agreed and Victor asked if he could talk to me privately, sure I said. We went into the bedroom and he began to tell me about Jesus, His soon return and end of the age. I would just nod at him and say something like oh yeah okay just to get him out because I wanted to get back to my party.

Victor came by many times to tell me about Jesus return and the end of the age. You know the crazy thing about it was; victor may have been doing a great job of sharing the gospel, but all I heard was, "Jesus is coming back and the earth is going to blow up and we are all going to die."

The spring of 1982 was a turning Point in my life, which would Also affect the lives of others around me. Little did I realize that though? I walked away from Jesus; HE never walked away from me.

In April of 1982 Jesus visited me for the second time. This Visitation caused me to return to the
Lord Jesus Christ with a fervent zealousness that still continues in my heart today.
The visitation started with the following scenes taking place: My fellow workers from the muffler shop and I were partying at a Southern American colonial style mansion. There was an abundance of drinking and carousing. I was participating fully when all of a sudden something started to bother my spirit. I did not understand what was happening, but I knew I had to ask God to forgive me for the lifestyle I had indulged in. Seeking privacy, I exited to a balcony overlooking a garden. I started to repent and tell God that I was sorry when I heard a voice say, "Forget it" I was startled and looked around to see who was playing a joke on me. Not finding anyone I continued to ask God's forgiveness. Again I heard a voice say, "Forget it." I looked around a second time,

finding no one. This time I was compelled to look into the sky. As I watched the sky an amazing thing happened. A strange but beautiful presence surrounded me as I watched the clouds change shapes. The clouds changed into a variety of different animals. A voice filled with love and peace spoke from among the animal shaped clouds. In my heart I knew I was talking with God. The voice proceeded to say, "Forget it, I want you to listen to my son Jesus, and if you can't make it grab onto one of the animals and it will bring you to heaven where you belong.1

    I reached up and grabbed the leg of the closest animal, which happened to be a lamb. Suddenly, I found myself running along a vast expanse of beach. Beautiful, peaceful, and exhilarating was this place was in. I looked out over a huge ocean and was aware that everything I could see was created just for me. I was totally amazed at surroundings, especially the peace I experienced.

Suddenly I was removed from that place and a new scene unfolded before my eyes. I could see a Jesus, standing beside a large rock, watching over his sheep. I walked over to where Jesus was and stood beside him and together we watched the herd of sheep. We watched the sheep together for a little while. We watched in silence not communicating with each other but totally aware of each other. I watched this scene with interest for few minutes. This scene disappeared and I was back at the balcony looking into the sky. Again the voice of the Lord spoke to me saying, "Forget it, all I want you to do is listen to my Son." At this point I made an unbelieving arrogant statement toward God. Why you might ask would a person make arrogant statements toward God. It is quite simple; being influenced in the occult and street gangs you are taught how to rebel against all authority. To my surprise He responded with authority and sternness, I sensed that if I didn't stop being ignorant my life could be easily finished at that point Even though God responded with sternness the great love He has for His creation never left His voice. Adamantly the Lord said, "LISTEN TO MY SON JESUS." After this statement the visitation ended.

1: Jesus was not telling me to forget about repentance. He was referring to my former lifestyle along with the guilt and fear. By saying forget it He was telling me that He wasn't holding my past against me. The Lord was implying also that I should forget about my past and Follow Jesus.

PHILIPPIANS 3:13-14,
"Brethren, I do not count myself to have apprehended; but one thing I do, forgetting those things which are behind and reaching forward to those things which are ahead, I press toward the goal for the Prize of the upward call of God in Christ Jesus."

At the time of this writing, many events and people have come into my life. I

have the sense of being called into two areas of the five-fold ministry, prophet and pastor. Am I a
pastoring prophet or a prophetic pastor? I guess time will tell as I trust the Holy Spirit to confirm His call upon my life.

16 CONFIRMATION OF THE CALL

I believe the year was 1984 and I had recommitted my life to the Lord in 1982 and my wife accepted Jesus in 1983. We were attending a small Pentecostal church relatively close to our house, more out of convenience than anything. My wife worked as a chambermaid cleaning hotel rooms and usually had to work some Sundays and couldn't attend church with me on a regular basis. I went to church as usual, not knowing that this day was going to be a pivotal day to change the course of my life. As I am writing this I just had the thought, "how many times do we have divine appointments in life that God has ordained to help us fulfill our destinies in Christ, and are totally unaware of them?" I was about to have such a divine appointment A little background information before I continue. At this time of my life diplomacy and kindness were not strong personality traits dominate in my life. These traits would be developed later in my life. Anyways I went to church by myself that Sunday as my wife had to work. I sat quietly listening to the message and just like most saints in the church was glad for the closing prayer. I stood up to leave and a native girl grabbed my arm and very rudely told me, not asked, but told me quite authoritatively that I was taking her home and coming in for a coffee. I was intrigued because no one talked to me like that because I would normally respond in like manner saying something like " who do you think you are ordering me around like that and I have better things to do!"

But nevertheless I said yes ma'am and drove her home and went into her home, which just happened to be the basement duplex my wife and I moved out of a month earlier. She introduced herself as Wynne and proceeded to make coffee while introducing me to her two children. Her and her husband and children had moved to Grande Prairie for work. Grande Prairie has always been a busy town for work. The saying around here was if you're not working it's because you don't want to. Back in those days it seemed like you could go to one business and apply for a job and if the owner didn't meet your requirements you could go next door and get the pay and conditions you wanted.

    Wynne and I began to talk about spiritual things, sharing our testimonies on the new birth. I became intrigued when she shared about the manifestations of the Holy Spirit and she was with a group of prayer warriors in central Alberta who had manifestations of Jesus in their lives. Wow I was hooked and wanted to know more because I had dreams and open visions of

Jesus when I was younger. It was a relief to find someone I could talk to about my experiences who wouldn't respond to me after sharing, "How much drugs did you take the night before?"

Wynne started talking about a subject I had little knowledge of," THE HOLY SPIRIT. "She asked me if I had been baptized with the Holy Spirit with the evidence of speaking in tongues." I proceeded to share with her sensing the presence of God many times and the open visions of Jesus and angels. I shared with her the trances the Holy Spirt gave me showing me His great love for me. As far as I was concerned I was baptized with the Holy Spirit. I was convinced by the Baptist religion I grew up in that you got everything including the Holy Spirit when you accepted Jesus as your savior.

Speaking in tongues and miracles all ceased after apostle Paul died because they were needed then because the church was just birthed in the earth and needed something to show that they were of God.

Any speaking in tongues today was a false sign and not of God. I really believed speaking in tongues was of the devil and I loved Jesus so much that I would have no part of a devilish deed. This I did not know was part of the cessation doctrine that says all the manifestations of the Holy Spirit stopped because we have the King James Version
of the bible. They use **1 Corinthians 13:10 when that which is perfect is come, then that which is in part shall be done away.** They use this scripture to justify why they have no power or manifestations of God in their midst. This is definitely a doctrine of devils meant to keep the church weak and powerless and at the mercy of the devil.
2 Timothy 3:5King James Version (KJV) 5 Having a form of godliness, but denying
the power thereof: from such turn away.

I did a google search and found the churches that are lacking in manifestations of the Holy Spirit are in decline while the churches that have manifestations of the Holy Spirit are growing.

But enough of the rabbit trail let's get back to Wynne. I presented my arguments to her justifying my position. She wouldn't back down, she stood eyeball to eyeball nose to nose fang to fang with me telling me that I wasn't baptized by the Holy Spirit but I was operating under the counsel of the Holy Spirit. Seeing she was a formidable foe whom I could not get to back down I graciously excused myself saying that I had to pick my wife up from work. When I got in my vehicle and drove about a block away I spoke really loud to God saying, "IF I DON'T HAVE THE HOLY SPIRIT I WANT HIM BECAUSE I WANT EVERYTHING YOU HAVE FOR ME."

I arrived at the hotel where my wife worked and explained to her that I met a really strange and unique woman at church today and she needed to meet her. We drove back to Wynne's house and I introduced the two women, they clicked right away and became fast friends. Wynne's husband worked out of town and she enjoyed the company. We continued to fellowship on a biweekly basis, learning about prophecy and other manifestations of the Holy Spirit.

    One evening she asked us if we were interested in a hallelujah party. We asked her what that was. She told us that we would go into the front room and begins to praise and worship God until He manifested in our midst. I never heard of such a thing. Sure we sing songs of worship and praise in church but that was out of duty and the program we are taught. A couple of fast songs then a couple of slow songs, an offering, then a forty-five minute sermon, which may or may not put you to sleep. Then the most anticipated moment of the whole Sunday church service came, the closing prayer and dismissal for lunch.

Wow praise God until He showed up, I was enticed wondering if it would work and how long would you actually have to praise and worship. We moved into the front room and began to sing praise songs and proclaim the blood of Jesus. After about half an hour I felt this peaceful presence enter the room, soothing warmth began to cover my head and flow down the back of my neck. My mind quickly turned off all natural thoughts and I could see Jesus walk into the room in my mind's eye.

Wynne moved beside my wife and asked her if she wanted to be baptized with the Holy Spirit. She said yes and Wynne laid hands on her and began to pray. Something unusual happened, my wife began to laugh. Every time Wynne would pray for her to receive the baptism of the Holy Spirit my wife would always break out in laughter. That wasn't the expected result. The bible gives us guide lines that we are to expect and follow.

Acts 2:4 4 and they were all filled with the Holy Spirit and began to speak in other tongues
as the Spirit gave them utterance.

The Holy Spirit Falls on the Gentiles
Acts 10:44 while Peter was still saying these things, the Holy Spirit fell on all who heard the word. 45 And the believers from among the circumcised who had come with Peter were amazed
because the gift of the Holy Spirit was poured out even on the Gentiles. 46 For they were hearing them speaking in tongues and extolling God.
Acts 19: And when Paul had laid his hands on them, the Holy Spirit came on them, and they began speaking in tongues and prophesying.

I admitted that I had some misbeliefs about God but when I read the truth in the bible, GOD'S WORD, my belief system changed. I also found out another truth.

Acts 10:34 King James Version (KJV)
34 Then Peter opened his mouth, and said, of a truth I perceive that God is no respecter of persons:

If God not being a respecter of persons baptized the apostles and the early church with the Holy Spirit with evidence of speaking in tongues then He will do the same for us today.

Luke 3:16 King James Bible
John answered, saying unto *them* all, I indeed baptize you with water; but one mightier than I cometh, the latchet of whose shoes I am not worthy to unloose: he shall baptize you with the Holy Ghost and with fire:

Matthew 3:11 New International Version
"I baptize you with water for repentance. But after me comes one who is more powerful than I, whose sandals I am not worthy to carry. He will baptize you with the Holy Spirit and fire.
Mark 1:8 King James Bible
I indeed have baptized you with water: but he shall baptize you with the Holy Ghost.

I am not greater than the apostles or the early church declaring that I don't need what they had. I need the Holy Spirit and His manifestations more today than ever before. We are living in the closing hours of the last days and sin is increasing and putting pressure on the body of Christ like never before. The Holy Spirit is preparing the Body of Christ for a supernatural end time harvest of souls and needs your participation in this event. Throw away the deception and misbeliefs that Satan has convinced you of and take the bible literally and watch the results. As I was saying my wife would break out laughing every time Wynne prayed for her. We decided to let it be and move on. We continued to praise God and enjoy His presence, having bouts of laughter for no reason whatsoever but really enjoying the overwhelming sensation of God's love.

Feeling tired we decided to shut it down for the night and maybe fast and pray for answers as to why my wife would break out in laughter every time hands were laid on her to receive the Holy Spirit. We started the praise about 10-10:30 pm and thought must be about midnight, time to go home and sleep. When we looked at the clock it was 3:30 am. Wow we were praising and enjoying the presence of the Lord for five hours, magnificent. We quickly got hooked on hallelujah parties and wanted more. A week later we got together again. We had spent the week fasting and praying while doing our daily activities. When we got together this time we were very focused in our praise and prayer. Last time being beginners we just shot everything out there hoping God would show up. He did because of His great Love for His children. We were baby Christians running around in our spiritual pampers so to speak. As we praised and prayed the Holy Spirit showed up and a word of knowledge manifested. The reason for the blockage was because of my wife's involvement in the occult that was never repented of. When my wife talked about it she usually had a look of satisfaction knowing that she could lift a two hundred fifty pound man off the floor by placing two fingers under him and lifting straight up with little to no effort. She realized her mistake and repented of the activity and never again had excitement over it but sorrow over it. I had never heard her talk about again. Wynne asked me to lay hands on my wife and agree with her in prayer for my wife to receive the Holy Spirit. As soon as I laid my hands on my wife I started speaking in tongues, a German sounding dialect.

    I looked out the window and realized we were in the presence of the Lord all night. The sun was starting to come up and I decided to go outside for fresh air. I went outside and stood on the sidewalk by my car. A very gentle breeze began to gust gently. I was amazed as to what I could hear with each gentle gust. I could hear the name of Jesus spoken very gently and drawn out.

JJJJEEEESSSSUUUUSSSS. As each gust came by I would hear the name of Jesus spoken in the same sweet drawn out manner. This continued on for about fifteen minutes. Needless I was excited and ran into the house to share my experience only to find everybody went to sleep after the night of worship.

I tried to sleep but to no avail. I was pumped up excited and wondering what manifestation of the Holy Spirit was that? I think I figured it out that it was a revelation gift, knowing that there may be 9 manifestations of the Holy Spirit, but you can categorize them in three different categories.

1. THE POWER GIFTS
A. GIFT OF FAITH
B. GIFTS OF HEALINGS
C. WORKING OF MIRACLES

2. REVELATION GIFTS
A. WORD OF KNOWLEDGE
B. WORD OF WISDOM
C. DISCERNING OF SPIRITS

3. THE SPEAKING GIFTS
A. SPEAKING IN TONGUES
B. INTERPRETATION OF TONGUES
C. PROPHECY

    Regardless of the category, I think people can get caught up into analyzing God to the point of missing the experience. I believe the Holy Spirit gave me this experience maybe just to show that He loved me and knew I would be tickled pink by it and would always remember it with pleasure and adonization for Him.

2 Corinthians 13:14 Berean Study Bible
May the grace of the Lord Jesus Christ, and the love of God, and the fellowship

of the Holy Spirit be with all of you. Out of that experience this poem or psalm as I would like to call them was written

NATURE

The birds, flowers and trees do sing
Rejoicing in the Lord their melodies ring
Watching the sun about half past five
When all of a sudden the breeze was alive
As the breeze continued on bye
The name of Jesus was exalted on high
As the anointing began to flow
A new revelation for me to know
Then one day while reading the Word
All excited over the phrase I heard
Sun, moon and stars of light
Praise His name this very night.

As I began to read my bible, especially the Old Testament about prophets, I was beginning to think, can we talk about this calling. I found the prophet's ministry interesting and a bit

exciting but the no failure; no mistake rule was a bit disturbing. Regardless of the non-error allowed rule when you got it right people didn't like you and tried to hurt you. I realized the first time I mentioned this call to a person I looked up to and got "TELL ME SOMETHING THAT IS GOING TO HAPPEN IN THE NEAR FUTURE AND YOU BETTER BE RIGHT." I learned real quickly that the prophet's ministry was not really accepted so keep it quiet what God is doing in your life. I decided the best
thing for me to do was to research this calling and ministry out for myself.

I read a scripture that gave me confidence in this matter and prayed for confirmation to this call of the office of the prophet.

2 Corinthians 13:1 Berean Study Bible
this is the third time I am coming to you. "Every matter must be established by the testimony of two or three witnesses."

I prayed in my heart, "I don't know enough of this ministry and calling so I will

wait for you to confirm it by two or three people who have never met and have no idea of each other." While I am waiting I will search this ministry out with all available sources at my disposal. I searched and searched and would only come across little pieces of information that gave some insight but would cause more questions. I did get my
confirmations a few years later. The second confirmation came from the two spiritual fathers I had who ordained me. I never told them about my call from the dream I had when I was ten years old or from Wynne. When they ordained me they publically announced their belief that God had called me into the office of a prophet. But before that happened let me share a rather humorous story of the first time I prophesied.

    I had been learning how to hear the voice of God in the mornings during prayer time.

**John 10:27 New King James Version (NKJV)
27 My sheep hear my voice, and I know them,
and they follow me.**

    I would get up around 5-6 am and go into the front room and pray. I would usually start with something like this. "Good morning Father, how's heaven today"? Then I would proceed to pray for king and country, my family and relatives and church meetings and anything else that would come across my mind. I continued this way for about a week.

    One morning I just got past my greeting of "Good morning Father how's heaven?" When I heard so loud in my spirit that I thought heard it audible with my ears. "HEAVENS GREAT HOW'S EARTH?" I was stunned into silence thinking how's earth? You are the all present all powerful all-knowing God and you ask me how's earth?

    He knew my thoughts and said "I am talking to you the same way you are talking to me." Wow, what a revelation, the God of the universe desires to fellowship with us that He temporarily sets aside His awesomeness in order to fellowship with us on our level. He approaches us where we are at but has a desire to raise us up eventually to His level. You may say impossible, yes with man but not with God. Anyways hearing God in private but speaking on His behalf in the form of a prophecy is totally out there and scary to me.

    Sitting in the church one Sunday morning I noticed we had an unusual anointing on the praise and worship which was exciting. About half way through the worship I started hearing words down in my spirit and I instinctively knew I was to start repeating them when there was a break in the music. I began to argue with the Holy Spirit which lasted less than a couple of seconds but in my mind seemed like an hour.

    I reminded the Holy Spirit who the pastor was, a one man show and everything was about him and I would probably get disciplined and maybe kicked out of the church. The Holy Spirit told me to say what He told me to say or He would make me stand up and apologize to the congregation that I had a word from the Lord and I refused to give it. Hahaha, you are thinking "God wouldn't do that, make you apologize." Have you forgotten what I mentioned about myself earlier? Diplomacy and kindness were not yet part of my development yet. The Holy Spirit knows how to get through to me to accomplish His will. I began to repeat the words I heard. I never got a paragraph or a book at once I just got a word and as I spoke each word another just fell off of my lips. It was an encouraging word of God's love and favor for the congregation. Something was taking place in that congregation I had never seen before, a freedom was erupting as a woman began to sing in tongues to my right another behind me interpreted the tongue sang in and another person started prophesying about the goodness of God. The place was a Holy Ghost fire pit and I chuckled to myself thinking "Thank you Jesus, he can't throw us all out." I learned a lot about walking in obedience in that situation. My family eventually moved to another Pentecostal church in town that was known for moving in the manifestations of the Holy Spirit.

Let's get back to the confirmation of two or three witnesses. The second witness was a revivalist from Saskatchewan. We had a few meetings with him the year before and it seemed everything was about laughter.

You get half way through a message and the congregation would burst out laughing. Not one here or there everybody would just burst out laughing. The praise and worship was phenomenal, the congregation wouldn't stop. The pastor would have to interrupt so the guest speaker could share the message God wanted to say for those revival meetings that were taking place in the late 90's. This revivalist came back early 2001 or so and we had another intense meeting. It wasn't so much laughter as before but more serious talking of a great awakening coming to the world and revival coming to a sleepy church. He would call people out of the congregation, prophecy over them or pray for healing after a word of knowledge. The people were blessed and encouraged to continue in the faith no matter what they were going through. I was watching the an event rejoicing with those who rejoiced and pleased that God was meeting the needs of the people. Suddenly he called me up and told me to raise my arms which I obeyed and he barely touched my forehead and the Spirit of God enveloped me and I fell forward into his arms. The ushers grabbed me and laid me on the floor and the most unusual vision unfolded.

    I found myself sitting with my back to a tree. This tree wasn't in the middle of a forest but sitting in an open meadow. This was a fruit tree of some kind, not like an apple or other hard type of fruit, but a soft fruit that you could squeeze it with your fingers and it would almost liquefy as it ran through your fingers. Jesus was sitting on the other side of the tree in contemplation. He stood up and had a broad smile on His face and plucked a piece of fruit from the tree. Jesus continued to walk around the tree to where I was sitting. As He got closer to me He began to chuckle harder and louder. In the vision I could hear my thoughts of wonderment, is it a riddle or a joke or a humorous story Jesus is going to tell me while we are sharing this fruit together? By this time Jesus was standing in front of me laughing and He bent down slightly as to sit beside me I thought when He did the most unexpected thing I could imagine. He squashed the soft fruit in my face and rubbed it in as it poured down my face. Then as quickly as the vision started it ended with that scenario. I picked myself off the floor and made my way back to my chair and sat down mystified to as what I had just seen.

After a few minutes and the revivalist ministering to a few more people called on me. "William, come up here come up here." I obeyed and proceeded to the front again. I stood in front of him and he told me to raise my hands and asked if I was ready? I said yes and thought to myself he will touch me and I will go down and maybe Jesus will explain that previous vision to me. He asked me again, "are you ready?" I said yes. He then told me to raise my hands higher. I did what he asked only to get asked again, "Are you ready?" Feeling a bit annoyed because I wanted to get back to that tree and have Jesus explains the vision to me. That of course is what I wanted to happen and thought it would. I was expecting a touch on the forehead like before and everyone else when came another totally unexpected thing like Jesus and the fruit. The revivalist open handed slapped me across the face with such force that I did a three sixty and landed on the floor on my face with no catchers catching me because they never seen that coming either. I was on the floor enveloped in a white cloud when the revivalist kneeled down and began to speak in a loud voice that God has called William Hatfield into the office of a prophet and that He, God was going to show His Glory through my face. Wow that not only explains the vision but gives me another confirmation of the call on my life. Okay now I am kind of excited thinking now I know why I am born and my purpose. Time to intensify my research of the prophet's ministry. I was in luck or should say rather blessed to find the church book keeper was running a home Christian book store. I found volumes of books on the prophet's ministry, ordered them and consumed them.

    One afternoon my friends and I heard of a prophet visiting a little church a couple of hours away from our city. Apparently he prophesied the church he was visiting into existence and named the pastors while the building was a broke down abandoned movie theatre. We went to that church for Sunday afternoon service and it started as church usually does. When the prophet began to speak it was an upbeat encouraging message. He then paused and pointed to my friends and told them things about their lives and children, which I can say at the time of this writing all has been fulfilled. He then continued with his sermon.

After about ten minutes he points to me and says, you have been called into the office of a prophet and you have a great ability to do research and God is going to use you to raise the dead.
Another confirmation to the call on my life. I pretty well settled the issue and decided to research and study and learn about the prophets ministry. I went to Bible College because they had a course on the prophetic. That was the only course of interest. I studied pastoral theology and the

other courses seemed tedious to me. The college had a test to show character traits which showed what ministry your personality makeup is best suited for. I scored 100% on prophet/perceiver and 100% on teacher and 85% on giver. I think I scored 60% or less for pastor. Even in the bible college the assistant dean recognized the prophet's ministry on my life. I also noticed the dean of the bible college also mentioned many times that I had a pastor's heart. He had noticed me sitting with other students helping them through issues in their lives. As I said I settled it in my life but I won't run around calling myself prophet because there is a lot of danger in that manly from people's misbeliefs and expectations they force upon you and I like a quiet peaceful life.

    Content to know why I am here on this earth and not interested in fame as I watched some self-proclaimed prophets run after only to find themselves on the scrap heap of life.

With all that said and done content to know and now study and learn to show myself a workman in the kingdom.

2 Timothy 2:15 New King James Version (NKJV)

15 **Be diligent to present yourself approved to God, a worker who does not need to be ashamed, rightly dividing the word of truth.**

Off to church I go not aware there is a special speaker from Alaska today. I was at this time running the sound board in church. The sound board was in the balcony where I could see the whole front of the church. This speaker was not the same old breed that we usually have and are today. It is hard to break out of our same old same format we have used for centuries in the church. Instead of having a sermon this speaker from Alaska began ministering in the Spirit immediately. Let me encourage you, this minister even though he had no sermon to preach ministered by the Spirit within the confines of the scripture. You could quote scripture for every prophecy and ministry he did to individuals. After a few minutes he looked up to the balcony and called me down. As I walked down the aisle he says "do you know why you are going through all the troubles and trials in your life? It is to get you out of the way because you are called into the office of a prophet and there can't be anything of you in that office only God through you." Icing on the cake, another confirmation but filling in the blanks to a lot of questions.

All these confirmations came in after Wynne and her family had moved east to Ontario.

They had no knowledge of her and she them nor did they know each other. Let me say something to you who may be called into the prophet's ministry. The prophet is gender neutral meaning it is an office that can be filled by either sex same as the teacher and evangelist. The only offices reserved for men is the apostle and pastor who have masculine connotations in their meanings and in the Greek both mean father. We see no evidence of female pastor or apostle in the New Testament.

    Anyways there is an order to the prophet's ministry. First the call which may be a supernatural dream like I had or maybe another prophet laid hands on you and declared that office to you. Just because you have the call doesn't make you the great prophet of God's man or woman of the hour. Second is the anointing which is the training period. This training period could take up to fifteen to twenty years depending on you and the area of ministry you will be released in. Third is the appointing when you will be released by the Holy Spirit to flow in the gifts placed in your life. God will confirm His Word spoken through your mouth with signs and wonders. Until then you are still in the anointing stage so just relax and grow.

Don't be impatient you will get there when the time is right and you are ready. Too soon and you will get hurt. We are all still in training and will never be out until after we are home with Jesus. Don't overlook the people who come across your path for it may be a divine appointment needed to get you back on destinies trail. Let me recap;
1. The call when I was ten.
2. Wynne prophesying the call
3. Spiritual fathers ordained the call
4. Revivalist declaring the call with signs
5. Prophet speaking the call with wonders
6. The Alaskan declaring the call with trials
7. Heeding the call and let's enter the anointing stage of growth and
training to be all that God called me
to be.
I have discussed point 6 with some people
and they have a hard time believing it.

In
Acts 9:16 New International Version (NIV)

16 **I will show him how much he must suffer for my name."**

I know this is talking about the apostle Paul and I by no means put myself on the same level as the apostle Paul. However I believe that if you are called of God into an effective ministry of building the kingdom of God and destroying the works of Satan, there will be trials. If Satan gets knowledge of the call I am sure he will do everything in his power to stop it. Anyways this is my story and I am sharing it to possibly give hope and understanding to many that may be going through similar situations in life. May you find joy in your journey to find the call on your life? May the peace of God consume you as you seek Him?

17 THE ANOINTING

1 john 2: 20 King James Version, But ye have an unction from the Holy One, and ye know all things.

1 john 2:20 New International Version: But you have an anointing from the Holy One, and all of you know the truth.

**New International Version
1 john 2:27 as for you, the anointing you received from him remains in you, and you do not need anyone to teach you. But as his anointing teaches you about all things and as that anointing is real, not counterfeit--just as it has taught you, remain in him.**

**King James Bible
1 john 2:27 But the anointing which ye have received of him abideth in you, and ye need not that any man teach you: but**

as the same anointing teacheth you of all things, and is truth, and is no lie, and even as it hath taught you, ye shall abide in him.

Firstly, what does it mean to *anoint*, the *anointing* or to be *anointed*? There are many Hebrew and Greek words in relation to anointing. But for the sake of study, I will only mention a few.

Anoint:

-Hebrew - verb

Mashach: To rub with oil, to consecrate and to paint.

Cwk: Pronounce 'sook': To smear over.

-Greek

Murizoz: To apply (unguent).

The Basic meaning of the word anoint is
simply to *smear something on an object.* Usually oil is involved, but it could be other substances such as paint or dye. This gives the idea that to anoint something or someone is an act of consecration.

-Hebrew - noun

Mashyach: 'anointed one' one who is consecrated for a special office or function? In simple terms, the anointing is the presence of the Holy Spirit being smeared upon someone. It is the overflowing life of Jesus which imparts supernatural strength enabling an individual to perform a special task or function in an office he is called and appointed to.

In simple layman's terms you cannot be taught legalistically to flow in any kind of ministry form. I know people who take 1 John 2:20, 27 and think that they don't have to go to church or bible study because God will teach them. These people usually come up with revelations so far off from the bible they end up wearing the label of fruit cakes and do more harm to the Christian faith than good.

Ephesians 4: 11 So Christ himself gave the apostles, the prophets, the evangelists, the pastors and teachers, 12 to equip his people for works of service, so that the body of Christ may be built up 13 until we all reach unity in the faith and in the knowledge of the Son of God and become mature, attaining to the whole measure of the fullness of Christ.

We have the fivefold ministry to help us grow up. To say we don't need them because I have an anointing is to reject the very word of God that declares that Jesus gave us them.

I am going to try to explain in anointing in my own words, how I understand it. There is nothing about the fivefold minister's that are like a form letter. Every church group is unique and they need a pastor who fits their temperament. The pastor has an anointing from God to work with the congregation to bring them to the fullness of Christ.

I believe the same thing goes for the prophet's ministry. We have local prophets, regional prophets, provincial prophets, prophets to the country and prophets to the earth. One prophet heralds the first coming of Jesus to a nation of Israel. There will be thousands of prophets heralding the second coming of Jesus to the earth. If God called you he will anoint you to teach you how to operate within the call. You cannot fulfill a spiritual call by natural means. To be honest it's not your great self that will stand before the judgment seat of Christ bragging about your great deeds you have performed in the flesh or natural realm. The person who stands before God willing to yield their lives to the Holy Spirit to be used in whatever area He wishes will receive the greatest rewards.

Matthew 10:39 King James Bible
He that findeth his life shall lose it: and he that loseth his life for my sake shall find it.

    Okay let's continue; I have watched people make up prophecies, copy other's prophetic words and regurgitate them hoping they will pass off for a prophetic person or maybe a prophet. This is silliness at its finest. You may get away with it temporarily but when the crunch comes, push to shove you will be revealed because you will have to stand by yourself. When your sponge is squeezed what's in there will come out and your true self will emerge.

Are you truly called, or a copycat, or a wannabe hoping to fake it until you make it. I have met people in these areas and they just give the prophetic and prophet's ministries, which are ordained of God to bless, edify and encourage people, a bad name and a sour taste.

18 EVIDENCE OF THE ANOINTING

I want to share a series of stories and events that have happened in my life. These events are probably not in chronological order, but in order as I remember them from the mid-eighties until now 2017. I will start with this event since I was just a couple years back serving the Lord. I think but not to be quoted about 1985 and I was learning about spiritual activity. Everything was great when my wife and I retired for the evening; WHEN it seemed like all hell broke loose, partying noise from upstairs, doors opening and closing by themselves, clock making loud ticking sounds after the batteries were out and had no power to function. Even a mirror lifted off the dresser and crashed against the wall falling to the floor in pieces. When I went to pick up the pieces I heard an audible voice say "touch those and I will cut your throat."

    Needless to say I backed off and decided to put a praise cassette to calm everything down. I mentioned partying upstairs; we have no tenants living in our attic. I had learned that praise and worship puts the enemy to flight so put on a praise cassette and everything should be fine. I was expecting everything to stop when the cassette began to speed up and the music became garbled. Fear engulfed me, my hair stood up and I grabbed my family and ran out of the house. I did not want anything to do with a haunted house. We went to my Cousin Victor's house and told him the story.

    Victor smiled and said okay let's go to your place and do something about it. My wife and children were spending the rest of the night so they are safe. I tried to back pedal because honestly I was scared and wanted nothing to do with that situation. My cousin, the big brave lion heart, would not let me alone, we are going. I agreed and when we got into the driveway I said, "You go first and turn on the lights and I will follow you." When we got to the door he said "the devil attacked you in the dark we are going to fight him in the dark." I thought you are welcome to do it and when you are done come get me I will be waiting in your car.

I followed Victor into the house and down stairs to the basement. He began to quote scripture and take authority over the devil and plead the blood of Christ over the house.

    I noticed that there was no retaliation from the enemy like I thought there might be. After all when you watched the movies the monsters and demons eventually lost but the good guys suffered wounds and maybe a fatality or two and I thought I was sure to be a fatality. After a few minutes there was peace in the basement so we headed upstairs where all the heavy activity occurred earlier. I was getting fear free and boldness came upon me as I followed my cousin. We continued to plead the blood of Christ when something extraordinary happened. I could see into the spirit realm and seen the devil or demon that had being causing problems in my house. It was about 5ft 7in skinny and ugly looking. To my surprise it was hiding in the hall closet and shaking like it was scared.

    I mentioned this to Victor and he came up with a plan of attack, attack and not retreat, the boldness was increasing exponentially. I would grab the closet door swing it open and he would lunge in and attack the demon. Side note:
Victor brought with him his big family bible which must have weighed a good fifteen pounds. We got into position, I am holding the hall door handle and Victor in

front of the door with the bible held over his head in an attack position. Our adrenalin was flowing as we were anticipating a massive free for all fight. Victor said okay and I pulled the door open with so much force that it almost came off the hinges. When I pulled it open something came out of the closet and victor lunged at it beating it with his words of rebuke and repeatedly hitting it with his big bible.

    Satisfied we were victorious and no demon would ever come near that house again but give warnings to his fellow demons to avoid that property unless they wanted to get a bad beating. We turned on the lights; remember we were doing this spiritual warfare in the dark. The light came on and revealed the item that fell out of the closet when I almost tore the door off its hinges. It was my wife's ironing board. Victor was rebuking and beating my wife's ironing board with his fifteen pound bible. I had to buy a new board for the wife. We looked at each other and giggled but I knew this for a fact I will never be in fear over the activities of the devil again. I had a revelation of the blood of Jesus Christ the most powerful force in existence.

Revelation 12:11 King James Version (KJV)

11 And they overcame him by the blood of the Lamb and by the word of their testimony; and they loved not their lives unto the death.

Before you judge us let me add that we were baby Christians who put on our big boy pampers and moved out in the revelation we had. I can really put my imagination to work and believe God the Father was watching his two children working together to defeat fear. I can really picture God the Father sitting on his throne and chuckling as Victor rebuked and beat the ironing board with his big bible.

I want you to notice something about verse eleven the blood of the lamb and word of your testimony is in the same category. Question to meditate, ponder and pray about. How important is my testimony?

My family and I returned home and found scriptures in the bible dealing with fear and soon conquered fear. The thing that struck me the most out of that was I seen into the spirit realm and knew where that demon was hiding. I believe that was the manifestation of the Holy Spirit called the Discerning of Spirits.

Another time I was in bed and ready to sleep after a tiring day. I closed my eyes and was drifting off to sleep when I sensed the presence of God strong around me. I opened my eyes to take a peek and could see Jesus kneeling by my bed just looking at me with a smile on his face. I just closed my eyes and had the most peaceful sleep in a long time. When I woke up the next morning I was thinking of a scripture I had read earlier that week.

Psalm 3:5 New Living Translation
I lay down and slept, yet I woke up in
safety, for the LORD was watching over
me.

I was thinking about how I would quietly walk into my son's room and look at him while he slept in his crib and imagine him growing up to do great things and be a person of great influence for the Lord. One thing I noticed was that a lot of personal encounters happen in the middle of the night.

I would wake up after an encounter to look at the clock and notice it is 3-3:30 am. Again I woke up about 3:00 am to see an angel walking slowly at the end of my bed through my bedroom. I looked at him and asked what are you doing here?

He stopped at the end of my bed and stared at me. He said nothing so I asked, "What is your assignment?" He smiled at me and walked through the wall. I thought how rude, he comes into my house and doesn't even say anything just walks through my bedroom. There you go natural carnal thinking to try and understand spiritual situations.

I prayed and asked God what had just happened and why. The Spirit of God said "I am showing you that the gift of Discerning of Spirits is now active in your life." The discerning of spirits is when your eyes are opened up to see in the spirit world. You see Jesus and the angels; you also see demonic entities as well. You can also discern the heart of a man. This gift is desperately needed by the church to protect it from charlatans.

Too many Christians fall victim to so called ministers selling green hankies and water from the river Jordan so they can get healed and untold riches. If the believer had the discerning of Spirit active they would reject this silliness, knowing their blessings come from Jesus and not hankies and muddy water supposedly from the river Jordan.

19 DREAMS

Let's take a look at dreams now. My second spiritual dream happened just shortly after the first one when I see the bible in the sky. This dream involved me flying in an airplane and then suddenly I was outside of the airplane looking in the window. I noticed a black box under the seat. Suddenly the black box exploded and the plane crashed. This dream happened three nights in a row. I never understood the dream but would turn on the evening news to hear about a plane crash with no survivors. I just thought maybe it's a warning not to fly in planes because they are unsafe. It wasn't until a few years later that I began to have understanding of dreams that I figured this one out.

    Dreams are parabolic in nature and are not to be taken literally. Flying dreams either in a plane or by yourself represent you being on a spiritual high after an encounter with God. Something dark or black in the dream represents an attack of the devil to rob you of the fullness of your experience. I was being warned that there was an attack coming which did happen and caused me to leave the church for a few years. You can read about it in my first book Repentance before Resurrection. I returned to the Lord through a dream as mentioned earlier in the chapter the call. I have had many dreams since then. One that stands out in my mind is dreaming of running on a large peaceful ocean shore and then diving into the ocean. I stayed under the ocean for what seemed like hours and never had to come up for breath. I swam around with the fishes, whales and sharks in a state of relative peace. I woke up the next morning thinking maybe God showed me my heavenly home, no the mansion but my back yard. Didn't he say in?

John 14:3
and, if I go and prepare a place for you, I will come again, and receive you to myself; that where I am, there you may be also.

    Since He knows how much I like swimming it would only make sense for my mansion in heaven to have an ocean size swimming pool. Again, natural carnal thinking to try and understand spiritual concepts, which didn't work. I believe I was being told that I was going to have a ministry among the nations represented by the ocean. I have been to the Philippines and had good success and have been invited back. I enjoyed the time there and look forward to other countries to minister in.

I have had dreams of churches that I have attended. I have attended a few churches after my spiritual father resigned and left his church to another pastor. I won't name the churches out of respect for them. Just because I don't fit in a particular church doesn't mean you don't. Maybe the reason I don't fit is because of the dream of Jesus and I watching a herd of sheep while standing beside a huge boulder was Him telling me that I will be an under shepherd to Him of our own congregation one day. I am totally open to that as I continue to find my place in the great body of Christ.

Two dreams about one church I was attending started with me wanting a little peace and drove out to a secluded area near a forest. The fresh smell of nature and birds singing was quite relaxing when I noticed two men approaching my car. The man on the passenger side reached in the window and grabbed my sunglasses. The other man came to my driver's door and tried to get in, but I locked it before he got there. I wasn't sure about being alone in the bush with a couple of large threatening men. I started driving away with him hanging from my door yelling he wanted my car. The dream ended. I went to my spiritual father and discussed the dream. The conclusion was the sunglasses represented the vision for my life while the car represented my life. So it was a warning dream that the vision God has given me for my life was in danger of being hijacked. The second dream about this church was I am in a buffet food restaurant with some friends when I noticed the pastor and his wife sitting at a table eating lunch. I excused myself from my friends and went to say hello to the pastor and his wife. When I approached the table I noticed the pastor's wife had a baby in her arms. I was asked to join them so I sat beside the pastor. After a few minutes of conversation the pastor grabbed me by the head and securely planted a kiss on my lips. His wife smiled and chuckled while saying, "you don't know when you are going to be kissed by a friend do you?" that dreams was easy but disturbing to interpret. The kiss was a Judas kiss of betrayal. The wife holding a baby represented the age of the church at the time of betrayal. I then remembered the time I first attended that church. My dreams and visions for ministry meant nothing and I would have to submit my life to their goals and dreams. If I wanted to be a part of their denomination then my dreams would be thrown away because everything was about them and no one else.

That's why we have many church organizations in the body of Christ. Each one has a unique role to fulfill and as believers we have to find where we fit. The last dream of a church was an interesting dream. Not a warning dream like other dreams about being involved in a certain church.

I enjoyed attending this particular

church, the fellowship was great. I enjoyed the men's group and bible studies we were involved in. I had a reoccurring dream, each one similar to each other but a little twist. The first dream was I was in a s.u.v and driving out of Grande Prairie heading west. In the dream I was aware that I was moving away rather than just going for a drive. I went to church the next Sunday and shared the dream with a couple of men. Their response was we don't want you to move, you fit right in this church and we enjoy your company. I decided okay I will stay because it after all was just a dream and the dream was to general. If I had an actual destination in the dream rather than west I would have thought differently.

Rabbit trail.... Years earlier I had a dream that I was to move to Guelph Ontario. My wife at the time was watching a program on television about people on the street and prayed "Please send someone to help those people." Little did she realize the Holy Spirit was dealing with me about BE PREPARED

TO BE THE ANSWER TO YOUR OWN PRAYERS?

I never knew the prayer my wife prayed but started having dreams of ministering to street people. I shared my dreams with my wife and she mentioned the television program and her prayer. Our ministry up to this point had been a coffee table ministry. What I mean by that is sitting in people's homes sharing Jesus over the coffee table or kitchen table. We seemed to attract the kind of people that really never fit in a well-dressed well-groomed setting. Church it seemed to these people was a religious adventure of hypocrites and legalistic judgmental people.

Anyways I dreamed one night the name of the city so we sold everything we could to get finances to go and left with our clothes only and a few ministry items. The crazy thing is we ran out of money before we got there and had to stop at a town many miles from our destination. I went into the social services to see if we could get help and they said no. I responded well I guess we look for a place here and we live here. As soon as I said that they cut me a cheque for a few hundred dollars and we continued our journey. We got to Guelph with little money left and went to a soup kitchen to eat and told them we had nowhere to live and boom we had lodgings for the night.

God worked everything out so we lived in a motel room for three months while we ministered to street people. We see people come to Jesus and start a new life. After three months the Holy Spirit said go back west. I thought we were heading back to Grande Prairie when the wheel fell off the utility trailer we were pulling at Saskatoon Saskatchewan. We spent three years in Saskatoon leading bible study and had two years of Bible College. During our time in Saskatoon we saw many hundred people come to Jesus as we ministered to street people, prostitutes and bikers. We eventually ended up back in Grande Prairie for work.

Okay back to the church. I decided to stay because I fit and got along with everyone. About a week later I had another dream of moving but this time I was pulling a U-Haul behind the SUV. I mentioned it again to the men and got the same response. I made the same decision to stay. After a couple of weeks I had a third dream. I was again in a SUV and heading west almost on top of Richmond Hill when I looked in the rear view mirror. In the rear view mirror I could see the Shekinah glory cloud of God settle upon Grande Prairie. In the dream the temptation to turn around was great because wow who wouldn't want to be in the middle of the Glory of God. The Spirit of God spoke loudly to me even if you see this don't go back because I am not there for you. I got the picture, when it is time to move I will go no matter what's happening where I am currently living. I believe the destination is revealed to me through different circumstances. Now that the destination is generally known now when God supplies the finances I will go. Two more dreams I wish to share. One involves spiritual warfare the other may have been a translation, I will leave that for you to decide. The warfare dream actually has its roots in an act of unknown disobedience of an impression I should have listened to.

   My wife and I went to bed totally healthy. I started dreaming that a 6ft 6in 250lb person wearing a black robe with a hoody covering his head came in my bedroom.

   I woke up in the dream to be aware this entity was a demon. I jumped out of bed and started punching him and said get out. I knocked his hoody off to reveal the head of a pig and fangs of a vampire. I said you are an ugly demon and I want you out of here. I continued beating him as the dream ended. I woke up the next morning in severe pain throughout my entire body like I had just

been in a bar room brawl. My wife, healthy the night before, was in agony from a sinus headache. I never gave the dream much thought until a few days later. I went to the doctor and he told me
that I had rheumatoid arthritis. This dream was about 2001. I made the mistake of agreeing with the doctor and accepting the condition. I accepted the illness claiming it as my own and could only talk sickness. This is the meaning of the dream; the pig head represented an unclean spirit as you can read the Old Testament and see the pig is listed as an unclean animal. The fangs like a vampire; a vampire sucks your blood from you.

Leviticus 17:11 New King James Version (NKJV)
11 For the life of the flesh *is* in the blood

The unclean spirit came to suck the life out of me. Arthritis just does that it slowly sucks the life out of you over a period of time. The reason I accepted it was because the doctor told me that it was inherited from my mother who had it. It was a genetic curse that jumped on me. You may say why didn't you rebuke it in Jesus name? Glad you asked.

Remember I mentioned an act of unknown disobedience of an impression I should have listened to. Jan 26 1997 I had spent the night in Edmonton and was getting up early to get home to go back to work. I got up and looked outside to see that it raining a little bit. It wasn't raining hard and I thought I could make it home if I drove slowly because winter and rain is not a good combination. I had a strong impression to stay for a bit and go for lunch with my brother Richard. I thought that would be great but I need to get back to work in Grande Prairie. I got dressed and ready to leave when I had another impression. Just wait for a little bit and go on the computer on a chat line and visit with someone. Again I thought okay that would be great but I really have to get back because my boss was expecting me. So I decided to go. After travelling a few blocks I did a brake test and realized it was very slippery. I decided if I travelled 10 kilometers an hour it would take three days to travel the three hundred miles back to Grande Prairie.

    After a few minutes the rain stopped and I did the brake test again and found I had traction. Quite pleased I picked up my speed as I noticed the sun coming out and drying the road. I continued through Edmonton, Spruce Grove, and stopped at Whitecourt for diner. Just outside of Whitecourt I realized it was slippery and slowed down only to get into a collision. This truck accident gave me a brain injury and post traumatic amnesia. It took me ten years to come out of that and in 2007 my mind suddenly cleared off and everything became normal again...

    I mentioned that to show you how Satan took advantage of my injury and kick someone while he was down. Since then I have learned spiritual warfare even in dreams. I went to sleep one evening to be awakened by somebody crawling into bed with me. Must be dreaming, as I felt the individual pushing on me trying to push me out of bed. I pushed back trying to push it out of bed. We continued pushing each other not making progress, neither one of us. It seemed we were equally matched. I decided to use words and rebuke it because words are more powerful that human strength. I started to speak I command you in and suddenly its hand covered my mouth. I forcefully removed its hand from my mouth and said get out of my bed in Jesus name and gave it a shove with my foot and it fell out of my bed. I decided to stomp it with my foot since it was on the floor. I stomped the floor but it was gone. I sensed something behind me. I turned to see this 9-10 foot tall creature behind me. I turned and stood up and said I command you to get out of my house in Jesus name and you can leave through the basement window. I walked forward it backed up; I continued walking forward backing it up to the small basement window. It started to leave through the window and I said I command you to leave in Jesus name.

The entity stopped and came back in and stood toe to toe with me. It had a smile on its face as it said "now you know I don't have to leave." I realized my mistake and said, "You have a choice, you can listen to me pray in tongues for three hours and worship the Holy Spirit or you can leave." When I said worship the Holy Spirit a disgusting look came over its face and it said Holy Spirit ugghhh. Then it just jumped through the window and out of my house. My mistake was I never believed my authority which became evident by having to tell the entity twice to leave. He sensed this and came back in. When I gave it the choice and ultimatum of worshipping the Holy Spirit it left because no matter how strong the devil likes to portray himself, they want nothing to do with the awesome creator. Satan was totally defeated by Jesus at the cross and wants nothing to do with the creator anymore.

When Christians get the revelation of the authority Jesus gave them through the cross and shed blood they will walk
in greater dimensions of spiritual authority. The next experience showed me this. Again I went to bed but my soul was a bit concerned so I went to sleep facing the direction the entity got into my bed. I thought if another one tried to get
into bed it wouldn't get in from behind. Soul can get into silliness at times. If an entity wanted to get into my bed from behind it would just go to the other side. But for some reason I never thought of that. Again, a dream or maybe not. I was standing by my bed and I was surrounded

by a python. The big snake was squeezing me. I struggled and struggled but felt it getting tighter. I rebuked it in Jesus name and I felt it begin to loosen on me. I struggled and finally got it from around me. I was holding it in my arms and pulling it off of me when I felt a pain in my back. It was intense like the snake had its teeth in my back and didn't want to let go. I said let me go in Jesus name and immediately it released me. As I held the snake it turned into a fluffy white cat purring gently in my arms. Its purring was trying to have a soothing effect on me. I thought no you don't I am not falling for that. A minute ago you were a snake holding me in bondage. I thought I am going to throw you outside. I proceeded up the stairs from my basement suite and opened the porch door to see two brown Rottweilers in the yard barking at me. I thought this should be fun throw the cat at the dogs and watch the dogs tear it apart. I threw the cat at the dogs and as soon as the cat landed it began to bark at the dogs. The dogs ignored the cat and continued to bark at me. I ignored the dogs went back in and woke up wondering about this experience.

The meaning of the dream is quite easy. The cat represented a familiar spirit that had kept me in bondage (the snake). A familiar spirit is a family spirit which brings curses from previous generation to the next. Rheumatoid arthritis has been a curse in my family for generations. The idea is said to be based on certain statements in the Bible. For example:

Exodus 20:5King James Version (KJV)
5 Thou shalt not bow down thyself to them, nor serve them: for I the LORD thy God am a jealous God, visiting the iniquity of the fathers upon the children unto the third and fourth generation of them that hate me;
Exodus 34:6-7King James Version (KJV)
6 And the LORD passed by before him, and proclaimed, The LORD, The LORD God, merciful and gracious, longsuffering, and abundant in goodness and truth,

7 Keeping mercy for thousands, forgiving iniquity and transgression and sin, and that will by no means clear the guilty; visiting the iniquity of the fathers upon the children, and upon the children's children, unto the third and to the fourth generation.

Numbers 14:18King James Version (KJV)
18 The LORD is longsuffering, and of great mercy, forgiving iniquity and transgression, and by no means clearing the guilty, visiting the iniquity of the fathers upon the children unto the third and fourth generation.

Deuteronomy 5:9King James Version (KJV)
9 Thou shalt not bow down thyself unto them, nor serve them: for I the LORD thy God am a jealous God, visiting the iniquity of the fathers upon the children unto the third and fourth generation of them that hate me.

This is the curse of the law for walking in disobedience to God's word and laws. There is a big but in the equation, and that is, when we accept Jesus Christ as our savior we are redeemed.

King James Bible Galatians 3:13
Christ hath redeemed us from the curse of the law, being made a curse for us: for it is written, Cursed *is* every one that hangeth on a tree:

2 Corinthians 5:21
God made Him who knew no sin to be sin on our behalf, so that in Him we might become the righteousness of God.

Here is the crux of the matter Satan through a familiar spirit attacked me with rheumatoid arthritis which has been in my family line for generations. At the time I was unaware of the benefits of the blood of Jesus even though I had been a Christian for decades. I accepted it not having the revelation that I was redeemed from it and the familiar spirit was attacking me illegally because I am no longer under the curse. The bible says in

Hosea 4:6 King James Bible
My people are destroyed for lack of knowledge: because thou hast rejected knowledge, I will also reject thee, that thou shalt be no priest to me: seeing thou hast forgotten the law of thy God, I will also forget thy children.

The familiar spirit kept me in bondage because of my lack of knowledge. The Holy Spirit gave me this dream to help me understand why arthritis had gotten me. I repented on behalf of previous generations back to ten generations. I do not want this curse to continue to my children and future generations.

Romans 8:2
"For the law of the Spirit of life in Christ Jesus
hath made me free from the law of sin and death."

The dogs represented mocking spirits and the cat barking at the dog and the dogs backing off from the cat showed authority structure in the kingdom of darkness.

I believe I am now free from family curses and it won't continue on to my next generation.

Thinking of the dogs, there may or may not be people who read this book and criticize it. Most people who critique and mock are full of misbeliefs or are of a dead religious nature. Carnal Christians can't handle supernatural events. Their minds just won't let them go there.

Romans 8:7 King James Version (KJV)

7 Because the carnal mind is enmity against God: for it is not subject to the law of God, neither indeed can be.

This next dream I would like to share is an instruction concerning other people. I attend a Thursday night bible study and we usually have many manifestations of the Holy Spirit. Two females stood out from the group that night and usually when someone stands out I usually write a psalm which is a prophetic poem for them. The meeting continued but all I had was a curiosity in me concerning these two individuals. I decided that I would pray about it at home that evening.

As I prayed I kept getting the impression that I was supposed to get oil and anoint them. I asked for a scripture because I won't do anything without the bible as my foundation. I kept thinking of when Samuel anointed David to be king and how he was the most unlikely of all his brothers. That actually fit these two because in the natural surely there is someone more charismatic, good looking, diplomatic and a people pleaser that would be a better candidate. I decided to ask God for a dream concerning the situation, simply because He talks to me quite frequently through dreams and visions.

This dream began with me standing in front of an easel with a canvas on it. I had a paint brush in my hand. Jesus was standing beside me. The two girls were in front of us but one more to the right side and the other to the left side.

Jesus would look at one girl then turn

to me and tell me what to paint. He then looked at the other girl and then tells me what to paint. Jesus continued looking at each girl a few times and in between each girl tells me what to paint. After a while a master portrait was painted. I mentioned to Jesus it was one portrait for both of them shouldn't it be one each. Jesus told me they have the same anointing but each will interpret the same portrait through different paradigms. I understood what He was saying; each woman was at different stages of growth and would interpret the portrait through the revelation of the Word of God that was in their individual lives. That was the confirmation I needed to anoint them the next bible study. I was instructed to use olive oil mixed with cinnamon powder to anoint Lori and Doris. Not necessarily their names but used for identity purpose rather than the two women, a little more closely to home. That being settled my next thought was anoint them for what? I was to anoint them to flow as prophetic teachers. I could see that teaching ability in each of them but the prophetic part was stronger in one of them. Both had prophetic anointing just one walked deeper in it than the other.

I am heavy on symbolism so I wondered why cinnamon mixed with olive oil. Cinnamon's figurative meaning from the Hebrew
The figurative meaning of cinnamon in the holy anointing oil can be taken from its Hebrew meaning "to erect or upright rolls." Also from its descriptive meaning *"sweet"* from the Hebrew being fragrant and spicy all rolled up into the spice of life that we find in living in the anointed life of the Lord Jesus Christ.

Olive oil can be a picture of the Holy Spirit, the One who sanctifies us, fills us, readies us to see Christ, and brings us light, joy, and spiritual health. Olive oil can also be seen as a symbol of the Holy Spirit (or possibly of faith) in Jesus' Olive oil was sometimes used as a symbol of richness, joy, and health.

Wow the Lord has a great plan for Lori and Doris and I get to anoint them for it. I was thrilled. I kept thinking of the verse

Jeremiah 29:11 New King James Version (NKJV)
11 For I know the thoughts that I think toward you, says the LORD, thoughts of peace and not of evil, to give you a future and a hope.
As Doris and Lori move in the anointing which is teaching them they are going to be more like Jesus and people will see Jesus through their lives continually. I went to the bible study the following Thursday and anointed them. I have watched them grow and develop a stronger more intimate with Jesus through the Holy Spirit as the years have gone by. I have had many dreams concerning different situations but I think you get the idea on how God can minister to you and through you this way. I want to take a look at visions in the next section.

20 VISIONS

What is a vision? The dictionary definition is

NOUN
1. the faculty or state of being able to see:
"She had defective vision"
2. an experience of seeing someone or something in a dream or trance, or as a supernatural apparition:
"The idea came to him in a vision"

VERB
Visions (third person present) _·_ **visioned** (past tense) _·_ **visioned** (past participle) _·_ **visioning** (present participle)
The meaning of vision, means what God shows a particular person of what may happen in the future, it could be in dreams or it could well be in showing the future while he is awake.

What is biblical definition of vision?

In the Bible, visions are instruments of

supernatural revelation. They are often means of communication, both visual and auditory, between Heavenly beings and people.

The meaning of Trance in the Bible (From *International Standard Bible Encyclopedia*)

Trans (ekstasis): The condition expressed by this word is a mental state in which the person affected is partially or wholly unconscious of objective sensations, but intensely alive to subjective impressions which, however they may be originated, are felt as if they were revelations from without. They may take the form of visual or auditory sensations or else of impressions of taste, smell, heat or cold.

    I gave you these two definitions to help you see that sometimes when in contact with heavenly beings you can experience an altered state of consciousness. In visions the Holy Spirit may reveal future things to you. When God reveals future things to you it is the revelation manifestation called the Word of Wisdom.

1 Corinthians 12:7 but the manifestation of the Spirit is given to every man to profit withal. 8For to one is given by the Spirit the
word of wisdom; to another the word of knowledge by the same Spirit.

The word of wisdom is a small piece of God's knowledge concerning future events. Not the complete but a partial piece of the future. The word of knowledge is a piece of God's knowledge concerning past and or present events. Not the complete but partial again. Both are revelation gifts the body of Christ desperately need in these end times. I want to share a vision where I was in a trance like state. I knew where I was but when the vision started I was totally consumed by the vision. All reality ceased and the vision was the only thing I was aware of. Instantly I went into a trance and a vision unfolded. Jesus was standing before me wearing the garments of a priest. We were standing beside a meadow with a creek running through it. Jesus bent down, picked a pebble from the creek and said, "You are like this pebble. I will clean you, shine you, and perfect you. Then I will place you back into this creek bed; this creek would not be complete without you." Then very emphatically the Lord said, 'I need you!'" The vision ended, I was totally thrilled at what I had seen. You are part of the Body of Christ.

God needs you, your church needs you, and I need you. Without you, the body is incomplete. I need you and you need me. Together we can function and see God's plans fulfilled in the earth.

The Holy Spirit through a trance gave me this vision to encourage me. Another vision that I have had repeatedly is; this one is not like a trance but more like looking in a window and watching it unfold. I find myself in the vision sitting in an open meadow up against a fruit tree. Jesus is sitting on the other side with his back against the tree same as I, in this vision I could hear very clear the words which were spoken, same as in the trance. Jesus said to me, "I will get you the bible college you think you need." I recognized a very patronizing tone in Jesus voice. I thought about this vision for a day or two then decided to go to Bible College. I did the third year and got my diploma in advanced teaching and pastoral studies. I received a lot of knowledge and was trained to think the way that denomination thought. Every denominational church thinks their organization is the right way. Everyone who is not like us needs to change because God has favor for my way of thinking thus saith me. By the time the year was up I was glad to go. I never attended graduation because my ride came four days early and I couldn't wait. I am not against Bible College. If you believe God is calling you to go then by all means go, and go now. My spiritual father had taught us so well that Bible College was just an expensive refresher course.

The Holy Spirit knew that when He gave me the vision. It wasn't more knowledge I needed but to develop a more intimate relationship with Him. The more intimate your relationship with the Holy Spirit then you receives wisdom
to apply the knowledge you have. I have had a few conversations with Jesus under that fruit tree and it seems that I meet him there when something important needs discussing.

My next vision involves a young woman who couldn't have children. We will call this woman Ashleigh which may not be her real name, but just to make it more on a personal level. We were at a bible study in a little town in northwestern Alberta when this young woman came up for prayer. Apparently she had been to the doctors and found out she wasn't able to have children. She wanted prayer for this. As we prayed the Holy Spirit gave me a strong impression that I was to hold my bible flat in my hand and she was to strike it three times. I held my bible flat and told her to strike it three times. She asked why and I said I don't know, just that I heard the Holy Spirit say to do it. She tapped the bible twice gently. Her grandma who is a godly woman said in a loud voice hit it hard. Ashleigh hit the bible hard the third time almost knocking it out of my hand. I was asked why and again I said I don't know but it is best to walk in obedience and trust God. We dismissed in prayer and after a little bit of fellowship I started the forty-five minute drive back to my home. About fifteen minutes from their house I had an open vision while driving.

An open vision is when you are completely aware of your surroundings and a vision like watching television appear in front of you. I was totally aware of the road and my ability to drive was still perfect. However in front of me appeared a vision of me what seemed like on a one hundred inch high definition televisions with five point one surround sound. I was explaining to Ashleigh the natures of her three children. The first two would be just like her because she was a gentle shy and slightly timid girl. The third however would be a person of strong influence who would influence many for Jesus.

    Remember Ashleigh struck the bible gently twice but when yielded to the influence of a godly woman struck it hard the third time. She in the natural made a declaration through her actions to the spirit world. Wow God was going to answer her prayer for children. I could hardly wait to go back to bible study next Thursday and share the vision with her. I shared the vision with the group and most kept silent. Ashleigh was sceptical to say the least. You could see in her eyes and countenance uncle you're crazy. We talked for a bit and she managed to stretch her faith and say maybe one but not three. During the week I had to visit her little town and chatted with her a couple of times about the vision. I noticed her thinking was starting to change as she would make playful jesting comments.

    Next Thursday bible study was a turning point. Most people fail to realize that they set the course for their lives by the words they speak. Ashleigh made the declaration that she was only going to get pregnant twice. She stretched her faith to two children. That's great, people have to have faith and believe for themselves. How do you know what people believe? Listen to their words that give them away and most people if not all actually walk out in their lives the words that they continually speak.

    A couple of weeks later Ashleigh told the bible study she had gotten pregnant. The group rejoiced and praised God with her. About a month or so Ashleigh went for an ultra sound and found out she was carrying twins. Life just continued on as normal and I would visit her once in a while encouraging her and even teasing her that maybe she might have a whole quiver of children. You could see in her stature that faith and belief were connecting. The evidence of the vision I had for her was coming to pass before her eyes. Many months had gone by and Thursday bible study was upon us again. Walking up to the house I met Ash on the sidewalk, she was talking to her aunt Lori. I had a strong impression of the number sixteen months. I mentioned this to Ash and Lori and they responded sixteen months in between the baby that's cool. Ashleigh gave birth to twin baby girls just like the vision said. The first two would be like her.

A few weeks later Ash text me and said she was pregnant. I responded with the words I heard in my spirit, "yes and he will be a boy and he is going to be a prophet before God." Needless to say after the ultra sound Ash confirmed it was a boy.

    She gave birth and fulfilled the vision of three children, two like her and the third one of strong influence. At the time of this writing the girls are eight and the boy is six. They are growing in Jesus with godly grandparents and relatives speaking into their lives. This godly mother stands before God in integrity and honor and raises her children to walk in the fear of the Lord as she does.

This next experience I want to share is unique. I put it in the category of visions simply because I am not sure. Was this a dream, a night vision, or an actual translation to heaven? I will share the experience and let you make your own judgment. I can so identify with what the apostle Paul was talking about in **2 Corinthians 12:21 King James Bible I knew a man in Christ above fourteen years ago, (whether in the body, I cannot tell; or whether out of the body, I cannot tell: God knoweth ;) such a one caught up to the third heaven.**

I put my head down on my pillow and closed my eyes and instantly I was in heaven. I was walking beside Jesus and noticed the expression on his face. It was an expression of solemn (not cheerful or smiling; serious) and concern mixed with sadness. We continued to walk until we came to a big iron door. We stopped at the door and I turned to Jesus and said, "You know what's in there." He said yes. I said, "It's the great white throne judgment." He said I know. I said, "Can I go in and watch?" He said; with a puzzled look on his face; "why do you want to watch that?" I said, "Because there is an aspect of our Father that no one knows and I want to know it." Jesus opened the door, let me in and closed the door behind me.

The room was dark and God the Father was clothed in a dark cloud. This room was a sad and foreboding place. Visually limited but emotionally enhanced. I believe that was because I was not allowed to see individual people but to feel the emotions of the event. I was there to see how this event affects God the Father not people. I was about to get a major revelation of the love of God for humanity. The emotions I felt were intensified more than I could ever imagine. The grief, sadness and utter hopelessness I experienced rocked my soul and entire being. The emotion I experienced was so intense that if it wasn't for the Holy Spirit protecting me I would be a crazy person in a mental ward today. The wild thing was it wasn't coming from the people being sentenced to the lake of fire. The emotion was coming from God the Father. After what seemed like an eternity I came out of the experience to find myself pacing in the front room. My bedroom is downstairs in the basement, how did I get upstairs to the living room? I don't know. I was pacing and emotionally a wreck. I was crying out in anguish to the Holy Spirit, "You are the helper please help Father because He is hurting." I turned my focus to God the Father and asked, "Why are you in so much torment? What is wrong?" God the Father responded, "My creation whom I love with all my heart forced me to sentence them to a lake of fire. I had no choice because they took all choice away from me. That decision tears me up. They forced me by rejecting the plan of salvation through the shed blood of Jesus."

What a revelation God is a God of emotion not a hard nose individual sitting on a throne in heaven waiting for the chance to judge us? God is full of mercy and compassion and the affairs of mankind are before him always.

Psalm8:4 New International Version
what is mankind that you are
mindful of them, human beings that
you care for them?

New Living Translation
what are mere mortals that you
should think about them, human
beings that you should care for
them?

English Standard Version
what is man that you are mindful of
him, and the son of man that you
care for him?

New American Standard Bible
What is man that you take thought of him, and the son of man that you care for him?

King James Bible
what is man that thou art mindful of him? And the son of man, that thou visits him?

Holman Christian Standard Bible
what is man that you remember him, the son of man that you look after him?

International Standard Version
what is man that you take notice of him, or the son of man that you pay attention to him?

John 3:16 New International Version (NIV)
16 For God so loved the world that he gave his
one and only Son, that whoever believes in

him shall not perish but have eternal life.

Romans 10:8-13, 8 But what saith it? The word is nigh thee, *even* **in thy mouth, and in**
thy heart: that is, the word of faith, which we
preach; 9 that if thou shalt confess with thy
mouth the Lord Jesus, and shalt believe in thine heart that God hath raised him from the dead, thou shalt be saved. 10 For with the heart man believeth unto righteousness;
and with the mouth confession is made unto
salvation. 11 For the scripture saith, whosoever believeth on him shall not be ashamed. 12 For there is no difference between the Jew and the Greek: for the same Lord over all is rich unto all that call upon him. 13 For whosoever shall call upon
the name of the Lord shall be saved.

PRAY JESUS COME INTO MY HEART FORGIVE ME OF ALL MY SINS. I BELIEVE THAT YOU DIED ON THE CROSS AND PAID FOR ALL MY SINS AND THAT YOU RAISED FROM THE DEAD. I BELIEVE YOU SHED YOUR BLOOD FOR ME TO CLEANSE ME OF ALL SIN AND I RECEIVE YOU INTO MY HEART AND DECLARE WITH MY MOUTH THAT YOU ARE LORD. ACCORDING TO YOUR WORD I AM SAVED AND WILL SPEND ETERNITY WITH YOU IN HEAVEN. THANK YOU JESUS: AMEN>

21 THE HEART

I am not discussing the heart as in the organ in our body that pumps blood through our system giving us life. I want to look at the central or innermost part of someone. There are many scriptures that mention heart but not as the physical organ. There are many Bible verses discussing the heart because God's word is clear that the condition of your heart is critical in your walk with the Lord.

Mark 11: 23 For verily I say unto you, That whosoever shall say unto this mountain, Be thou removed, and be thou cast into the sea; and shall not doubt in his **heart**, but shall believe that those things which he saith shall come to pass; he shall have whatsoever he saith. This is the heart I want to look at.

Matthew 6:**21** For where your treasure is, there your heart will be also.

Proverbs 3:**5** Trust in the LORD with all your heart and lean not on your own understanding;

Proverbs 4:23 Above all else, guard your heart, for everything you do flows from it.

Romans 12:2 Do not conform to the pattern of this world, but be transformed by the renewing of your mind. Then you will be able to test and approve what God's will is—his good, pleasing and perfect will.

Proverbs 23:26 My son, give me your heart and let your eyes delight in my ways,

Psalm 51:10 Create in me a pure heart, O God, and renew a steadfast spirit within me.

Psalm 73:26 My flesh and my heart may fail, but God is the strength of my heart and my portion forever.

Philippians 4:7And the peace of God, which transcends all understanding, will guard your hearts and your minds in Christ Jesus.

John 14:27 Peace I leave with you; my peace I give you. I do not give to you as the world gives. Do not let your hearts be troubled and do not be afraid.

Psalm 37:4 Take delight in the LORD, and he will give you the desires of your heart.

Job 9:4 His wisdom is profound, his power is vast. Who has resisted him and come out unscathed?

Psalm 9:1 I will give thanks to you, LORD, with all my heart; I will tell of all your wonderful deeds.

Psalm 26:2 Test me, LORD, and try me, examine my heart and my mind;

Psalm 34:18 The LORD is close to the broken-hearted and saves those who are crushed in spirit.

Matthew 5:8 Blessed are the pure in heart, for they will see God.

Mark 6:52 for they had not understood about the loaves; their hearts were hardened.

Psalm 24:4 The one who has clean hands and a pure heart, who does not trust in an idol or swear by a false god.

Psalm 19:14 May these words of my mouth and this meditation of my heart be pleasing in your sight, LORD, my Rock and my Redeemer.

Psalm 119:1 Blessed are those whose ways are blameless, who walk according to the law of the LORD.

If the condition of our hearts were not important to God there wouldn't be this many scriptures dealing with it. I use to think that our hearts were our spirits which at the new birth is perfect in the sight of God and sinless. But the terms broken-hearted hard hearted doubt in heart pure in heart makes me wonder.

Word study mode kicks in so look up in strong concordance meaning of heart in mark 11:23

2588. kardia ▶

Strong's Concordance

kardia: heart

Original Word: καρδία, ας, ἡ
Part of Speech: Noun, Feminine
Transliteration: kardia
Phonetic Spelling: (kar-dee'-ah)
Definition: heart
Usage: lit: the heart; mind, character, inner self, will, intention, center.

HELPS Word-studies

2588 *kardía* – *heart*; "the *affective* center of our being" and the *capacity of moral preference* (*volitional desire, choice*; see P. Hughs, *2 Cor*, 354); "*desire*-producer that makes us tick" (G. Archer), i.e. our "*desire-decisions*" that establish who we really are.

[*Heart* (2588 /*kardía*) is mentioned over 800 times in Scripture, but *never* referring to the literal physical pump that drives the blood. That is, "heart" is *only used figuratively* (both in the OT and NT.

Interestingly sheds a whole new light on

things. Let's continue our research and study to see if we can get revelation and blessing to invade our lives.

22 OPINIONS

Opinions, this is something everyone has and is quick to express theirs. I heard a preacher once say God is not interested in our opinions. I don't get offended at such comments because when I hear them I automatically think, "of course He don't, He is all knowing all seeing and unlimited and I barely have a clue about my own sphere of influence." That's surface thinking and put's God beyond the scope of having a relationship with me. So I decided to look at it again with relationship between creator and creation in mind.

First thing I asked myself was where do opinions come from? Opinions come through interaction with others within the sphere of our influence. They come through our five senses. Humans have a multitude of **senses.** Sight, hearing, taste, smell, and touch are the **five** traditionally recognized.

Then I clued in God wasn't in the equation and probably eighty to ninety percent of our opinions are formed from the lower kingdom the natural fallen world. In our relationship with the Holy Spirit who is in the earth today leading guiding and brings revelation, He desires a change to happen in us. I want to share an event that happened to me as a young Christian to help me understand speaking from the lower kingdom.

I would get up very early in the morning before anyone else. The living room was a quiet deserted and comfortable place to pray. I would start my prayers with, "good morning Father God how's heaven." Then I would pray for pastor's government leader's family and neighbors. I had a routine of this day after day. Then one morning after I asked the heavenly Father how's heaven? He quickly responded "heaven's great how is earth? "I was stunned and didn't pray that day. Instead I asked older Christians why God would ask me that. I got a lot of religious sounding opinions that never settled in my thinking. So being super intelligent and wise (hahaha) I did what I should have done firstly. I asked God why did you ask me how is earth? He responded, "I was talking to you the same way you were talking to me. You asked me how is heaven so I asked you how is earth." Then suddenly an epiphany or revelation hit my mind 2 Peter 1: [19] **We also have the prophetic message as something completely reliable, and you will do well to** pay attention to it, as to a light shining in a dark place, until the day dawns and the morning star rises in your hearts

    I understood God comes to us on our level with the intent of ringing us up to his level.

We can be at another level when it comes to expressing our opinions. How you may ask? James 1:19 Know this, my beloved brothers: let every person be quick to hear, slow to speak, slow to anger; So hear what people say and be quick to turn inwards seeking counsel and wisdom from the Holy Spirit before expressing your opinion.

Hebrews 5:12-14 [12]In fact, though by this time you ought to be teachers, you need someone to teach you the elementary truths of God's word all over again. You need milk, not solid food! [13]Anyone, who lives on milk, being still an infant, is not acquainted with the teaching about righteousness. ¹⁴But solid food is for the mature, who by constant use have trained themselves to distinguish good from evil.

23 CHARACTER

There are many meanings of character but I want to use this one for our study.

Character
[ˈkerəktər]
NOUN
1. The mental and moral qualities distinctive to an individual.
   "running away was not in keeping with her character"
   synonyms:
   personality · nature · disposition · temperament · temper · mentality · turn of mind · psychology · psyche · constitution · makeup · make · stamp · mold · cast · persona · attributes · features · qualities · properties · traits · essential quality · essence · sum and substance · individuality · identity · distinctiveness · uniqueness · spirit ·

<u>ethos</u> · <u>complexion</u> · <u>key</u> · <u>tone</u> · <u>tenor</u> · <u>ambience</u> · <u>air</u> · <u>aura</u> · <u>feel</u> · <u>feeling</u> · <u>vibrations</u> · <u>kidney</u> · <u>humor</u> · <u>grain</u>

We have been given a new nature at the born again experience.

2 Corinthians 5: **17**Therefore, if anyone is in Christ, he is a new creation. The old has passed away; behold, the new has come. **18**All this is from God, who through Christ reconciled us to himself and gave us the ministry of reconciliation; **19**that is, in Christ God was reconciling the world to himself, not counting their trespasses against them, and entrusting to us the message of reconciliation. **20**Therefore, we are ambassadors for Christ, God making his appeal through us. We implore you on behalf of Christ, be reconciled to God. **21**For our sake he made him to be sin who knew no sin, so that in him we might become the righteousness of God.

We are a new creation so the old sin nature should not dominate our thinking or actions, but yet the old nature seems to rear its ugly head now and again.

Romans 7:15-20 New International Version (NIV)
15 I do not understand what I do. For what I want to do I do not do, but what I hate I do. **16** And if I do what I do not want to do, I agree that the law is good. **17** As it is, it is no longer I myself who do it, but it is sin living in me. **18** For I know that good itself does not dwell in me, that is, in my sinful nature.[a] For I have the desire to do what is good, but I cannot carry it out. **19** For I do not do the good I want to do, but the evil I do not want to do—this I keep on doing. **20** Now if I do what I do not want to do, it is no longer I who do it, but it is sin living in me that does it.

Problem, problem, problem because the bible says we are like Christ.

1 John 4:17 King James Bible
Herein is our love made perfect, that we may have boldness in the day of judgment: because as he is, so are we in this world.

When I look at myself and judge myself I don't act or look like Christ. How can I change to be more like Jesus Christ?

24 THE MIND

The mind or our thinking centre has to change drastically.

Romans 12 New International Version (NIV)

A Living Sacrifice

12 Therefore, I urge you, brothers and sisters, in view of God's mercy, to offer your bodies as a living sacrifice, holy and pleasing to God—this is your true and proper worship. **²** Do not conform to the pattern of this world, but be transformed by the renewing of your mind. Then you will be able to test and approve what God's will is—his good, pleasing and perfect will.

Our thinking patterns so determine our actions.

Romans 8:6 Contemporary English Version
If our minds are ruled by our desires, we will die. But if our minds are ruled by the Spirit, we will have life and peace.

I lived with a Christian couple for a while and noticed different behavior from what I thought should be norm. Every night after supper the television would come on and would put on a movie that included blasphemy sexual situations and an abundance of violence. I would retire to my room and watch preaching on you tube. One evening I tried putting on a godly show and the man hollered turn that garbage off. I was glad when I was able to move from that place.

What is Jesus to us? We get born again our fire insurance so as to not be thrown into the lake of fire at judgment day, then forget about a relationship with the Holy Spirit? Live our lives according to our natural lustful desires and when we begin to reap the rewards that come with the lifestyle of being carnally minded we run to God for help. In God's mercy he helps us so we thank him and act all religious, maybe take in an extra service we normally don't attend. Then after a period of time we forget and go back to the carnal thinking that got us to the place we didn't want to be.

Romans 8:6-7 King James Version (KJV)

⁶ For to be carnally minded is death; but to be spiritually minded is life and peace.

⁷ Because the carnal mind is enmity against God: for it is not subject to the law of God, neither indeed can be.

So my question to you is how important do you **think you're thinking patterns are in your relationship with God and people?** What are you going to do to be spiritually minded rather than carnal minded?

25 MY WILL_MOTIVES

My will! The most important will in life. I want things done my way. I want everything my way. I want all people within the sphere of my influence to bow down to my will. Everything in life is about me. Prosperity, health, honor and especially fame and accolades all about me. This is basically the carnal nature at its finest. As Christians we are not exempt from this.

Here is a thought about the definition of time; TIME IS WHEN TWO OPPOSING WILLS ARE IN MOTION AT THE SAME INSTANCE.

Jeremiah 17:9 [9]**The** heart is deceitful above all things and beyond cure. Who can understand it?

My will and my motives come from my heart. I can do acts of charity and kindness and look good in the eyes of men who don't know why I did them. I know of a situation where a person needed a place to live and another person offered him a bedroom to live for the price of a book. When asked why so cheap the man responded so my dad can't stay here on the weekends like he wants to. After a couple of months the demand for money came and it became higher and higher. It became apparent the man didn't want to work and was looking for someone else to pay his mortgage while he sat around visiting with friends. He couldn't find a boss that would submit to his will which dictated the days and hours and type of work he wanted because after all he was a child of God and he had authority over the dark kingdom. You can imagine the jobs he went through. Sad thing this was done in front of church members and bible study groups to show how good and charitable he was. Renting the room out for the price of the book was what was told everyone in the beginning so as to look good in people's eyes. The rest of his actions were done privately and secretly. Our hearts can be so deceptive that our motives though looking good on the outward can be really self-serving and manipulating.

Many times we judge others by their actions while judging ourselves by our intentions.

How can we be free from such attitudes of self-serving and judgments? When my will and motives rule then truth is lost and self-deception reigns rampant.

I wonder what the Lord's Prayer has to say about my will Luke 11 King James Version (KJV) **11** And it came to pass, that, as he was praying in a certain place, when he ceased, one of his disciples said unto him, Lord, teach us to pray, as John also taught his disciples.

² And he said unto them, when ye pray, say, Our Father which art in heaven, Hallowed be thy name. Thy kingdom come. Thy will be done, as in heaven, so in earth.

³ Give us day by day our daily bread.

⁴ And forgive us our sins; for we also forgive every one that is indebted to us. And lead us not into temptation; but deliver us from evil.

The Father's will be done not my will. What about Jesus in the garden?

Matthew 26:36-41 Then Jesus went with his

disciples to a place called Gethsemane, and he said to them, "Sit here while I go over there and pray." 37 He took Peter and the two sons of Zebedee along with him, and he began to be sorrowful and troubled. 38 Then he said to them, "My soul is overwhelmed with sorrow to the point of death. Stay here and keep watch with me." 39 Going a little farther, he fell with his face to the ground and prayed, "My Father, if it is possible, may this cup be taken from me. Yet not **as I will**, but as **you will**." 40 Then he returned to his disciples and found them sleeping. "Could you men not keep watch with me for one hour?" he asked Peter. 41 "Watch and pray so that you will not fall into temptation. The spirit is willing, but the body is weak."

Life isn't about my will but the father's will. How do we make that happen?

 The answer starts with this verse.   James 4:7 New King James Version
Therefore submit to God. Resist the devil and he will flee from you.

When we submit to the Holy Spirit we give Him permission in us to change us into the image of Jesus.

1Corinthians 4:5 ⁵Therefore judge nothing before the appointed time; wait until the LORD comes. He will bring to light what is hidden in darkness and will expose the motives of the heart. At that time each will receive their praise from God.

Sometimes people come into our lives and show us what not to be like. Other times people give us inspiration to grow in our relationship with the Holy Spirit.

26 OPENING THE BOOK OF YOUR HEART

Opening my heart seems scary for some people. Open up your heart in marriage only to be betrayed and used. Never measuring up to people; always falling short. Can I be sure God won't reject me like some people do? When we become children of God everything changes. We become children of a God who doesn't have love but is love. The entire passage found in 1 John 4:7-21 speaks of God's loving nature. Love is not merely an attribute of God, it is his very nature. God is not only loving, he is fundamentally love. God alone loves in the completeness and perfection of love.

Thus, if God is love and we, his followers, are born of God, then we will also love. God loves us, so we must love one another. A true Christian, one saved by love and filled with God's love, must live in love toward God and others.

In this section of Scripture, we learn that brotherly love is our response to God's love. The Lord teaches believers how to show his love to others, to our friends, family, and even our enemies. God's love is unconditional; his love is very different from the human love we experience with one another because it is not based on feelings. He doesn't love us because we please him. He loves us simply because he is love.

Love is the true test of Christianity. The character of God is rooted in love. We receive God's love in our relationship with him. We experience God's love in our relationships with others.

God's love is a gift. God's love is a life-giving, energizing force. This love was demonstrated in Jesus Christ: "As the Father has loved me, so have I loved you.

Abide in my love" (John 15:9, ESV). When we receive God's love, we are enabled through that love to love others. Satan tries to instill fear in us to prevent us from opening our hearts to God.

2 timothy 1:7 King James Bible
For God hath not given us the spirit of fear; but of power, and of love, and of a sound mind.

Christian Standard Bible
For God has not given us a spirit of fear, but one of power, love, and sound judgment.

Contemporary English Version
God's Spirit doesn't make cowards out of us. The Spirit gives us power, love, and self-control.

Satan continually puts thoughts in our head of failure rejection and failure. These thoughts are on replay and will continue over and over again until you do something about them.

2 Corinthians 10:5-7 King James Version (KJV)

⁵ Casting down imaginations, and every high thing that exalteth itself against the knowledge of God, and bringing into captivity every thought to the obedience of Christ;

I asked a brother in Christ how his relationship with the Holy Spirit was going and he responded, "As I yield and submit my heart more, more and more the relationship is improving."

Romans 12:2 ESV

Do not be conformed to this world, but be transformed by the renewal of your mind, that by testing you may discern what is the will of God, what is good and acceptable and perfect.

Ephesians 1:18

Ephesians 1:18 Having the eyes of your hearts enlightened, that you may know what is the hope to which he has called you, what are the riches of his glorious inheritance in the saints,

1. That should be our daily prayer. Pray in the Spirit. "But you, beloved, building yourselves up in your most holy faith and praying in the Holy Spirit...**Jude 1:20**
2. Fully trust the Lord. "... keep yourselves in the love of God, waiting for the mercy of our Lord Jesus ... **Jude 1:21**
3. Cultivate Christ's heart. "And have mercy on those who doubt; save others by snatching them out ... Jude 1:22-23
4. Have the fear of God. "... to others show mercy with fear..." (Jude 23) In our drive to rescue others ...

We are in a war and Satan knows that if we open the book of our heart to God we become an unconquerable enemy blessed by God.

THE MESSAGE BIBLE PSALM 18:24

God rewrote the text of my life when I opened the book of my heart to his eyes.

25 The good people taste your goodness; the whole people taste your health,

26 The true people taste your truth; the bad ones can't figure you out.

27 You take the side of the down-and-out, but the stuck-up you take down a peg.

28 Suddenly, God, you floodlight my life; I'm blazing with glory, God's glory!

27 WORDS AND DESTINY

People don't realize how important words spoken are.

Luke 6:45 English Standard Version
The good person out of the good treasure of his heart produces good, and the evil person out of his evil treasure produces evil, for out of the abundance of the heart his mouth speaks.

What people fail to realize is that you will eventually walk and live what you talk. If your heart is good you will speak life and blessing to all within the sphere of your influence.

WORDS

Words! It is totally amazing that this subject is probably one of the most taught subjects, yet the Body of Christ is still grossly ignorant of the effect words have in our lives. It is time to wake up and realize what is happening here. In the following dream we are going to see the importance and power of words and why Satan would like to control your tongue. This dream started with my wife Carrie and me walking up the sidewalk on our way to church. Upon entering the lobby of the church we noticed the Pastor standing a few feet inside the sanctuary. We thought this was rather strange as the pastor was usually in the lobby greeting people. The pastor was bidding people to come into the sanctuary and take a seat. The look on the pastor's face was very different than the joyful expression he usually carted around. You could see fear in his eyes and a slight trembling of his body. I was wondering why the other people who were filing into the sanctuary were totally oblivious to the pastor's nervous apprehension.

Soon the entire congregation was seated. The pastor made his way to the pulpit and began to speak. About a minute into the pastor's message a sound echoed throughout the sanctuary. The sound was the sound of rifle bolts being snapped into place arming the weapons. I turned around to see the source of the sound. In the balcony of our church were people holding guns of all kinds. They were carrying rifles, shotguns, machine guns, and a variety of other high-powered weapons. This group of people was holding the entire church captive. There were only a few gunmen but the entire congregation sat in fear of these men. These men told the congregation to sit quietly or else they would be shot. I looked around the church and everyone was paralyzed with fear.

Suddenly I began to quote scriptures from the bible. I quoted Isaiah 54:17, "No weapon formed against you shall prosper, and every tongue which raises against you in judgment you shall condemn. This is the heritage of the servants of the Lord, and their righteousness is from me, says the Lord." I also quoted Luke 10:19, "Behold, I give you the authority to trample on serpents and scorpions, and over all the power of the enemy, and nothing shall by any means hurt you."

I quoted these scriptures three or four times, and then I stood to my feet. Turning to face our captors, I continued quoting scriptures. The gunmen started shouting and hollering for me to sit down and shut up or else I would be shot. I use the term gunmen here in a most generic term not implying just males but including females in the term as well. I started to make my way to the balcony still quoting scriptures. I yelled the scriptures so loud, in response to their threats that I blocked out the sounds they were making.

These scriptures exploded in my heart becoming so powerful and overwhelmed me to the degree that the truths they portrayed became the only thing I could comprehend or understand.

The gunmen opened fire upon me with every weapon they had. I kept quoting Isaiah 54:17 and Luke 10:19 as the bullets bounced off my chest. The men were really surprised to see that their weapons had no effect on me. I proceeded to the balcony, disarmed them, and brought them down to the front of the church.

The pastor started preaching with enthusiasm and fire from the core of his being as the gunmen were coming down the aisle toward the front of the church. When the gunmen got to the front of the church the pastor became unglued, preaching with everything he had in him. The Anointing of God was released and after a few minutes some of the gunmen broke down and repented for their actions against the church. When we enquired of the remaining gunmen as to whether or not they would like to repent demonic spirits began to manifest through them. We commanded the devils to leave in the name of Jesus Christ. After the devils left the remaining gunmen repented. This was the end of the dream.

The interpretation of the dream is this; the gunmen are Christians, the rifles and high-powered weapons are the Christian's tongues; the bullets are **WORDS.** The Christians in the balcony represent their position of spirituality they thought they had attained. They believed they were greater in their walk with God than anyone else. They exalted themselves above measure simply because they had an office or a position or title in the church. Their words brought fear and bondage upon all who heard them speak in the church. This was easily accomplished by having the congregation believe their exalted position.

When I stood up and challenged them they felt threatened, unleashing words meant for my destruction. The scriptures I quoted not only protected me but also disarmed them. These people were using their tongues to control the church. By creating an atmosphere of fear and bondage the church remained paralyzed. The Holy Spirit wasn't able to move the way He wanted to in this church because when He would move He be spoken against, especially if it wasn't the way the gunmen thought it should be. The Holy Spirit is a gentleman and will not include us in His moves if we don't want to be involved. He will pass over us and let us have our fear and bondage if we want it. After being brought down from their lofty perch, they were escorted to the front of the church. The pastor preached God's word with authority and power because he himself was set free when these people were removed from their lofty perch. After hearing the Word of God many repented while others had to have the devil cast off of them. Once the devil was gone then all could repent and be set free from their patterns of destruction they were causing.

I believe and have seen this sort of activity happening in many churches today. Some of the people who use their tongues for destruction are simply ignorant of the harm they are doing. When they are quiet long enough to hear God's voice manifested through His Word they will repent. You may have to challenge them to change. We also have those who are so caught up with religion and tradition that blindness has come upon them in part. This type of people looks to the past. When God moved a certain way back then and they had an experience with Him they seem to think that that is the only way God moves and speak against any new thing He may be attempting to do in their church. They like their comfort zones and continually thwart the plan of God by using demeaning destructive words to stop the move of God in their church.

When I realized words play an important part in my life I began to seek the Lord and ask for revelation in this area. Out of the abundance of my heart my tongue will utter and eventually my feet will walk what I talk. Your actions will soon show the world and God what's in your heart. Paul said in **1 Corinthians 11:1** Be imitators of me, even as I also am of Christ. **Philippians 3:17** Join one another in following my example, brothers, and carefully observe those who walk according to the pattern we set for you.

I realized there is a pattern we could follow to be an example of Christ in us and words can create that pattern.

Mark 11:23 [23]"Truly I tell you, if anyone says to this mountain, 'Go, throw yourself into the sea,' and does not doubt in their heart but believes that what they say will happen, it will be done for them.

The mountain in this case is the

condition of my heart; if I chose to believe the words that come from my mouth I can change the condition of my heart. I read the old testament many times and I noticed when the kings spoke words well or bad it affected his entire kingdom. I also noticed when God was going to talk with people He would speak about His character first then what He said was manifested. Hmmm I thought if we are to imitate Christ then what words should I speak in order to have Christ in me manifested rather than carnal flesh me?

I studied the fruit of the Spirit; **Galatians 5:22-26** ^{22}But the **fruit of** the Spirit is love, joy, peace, forbearance, kindness, goodness, faithfulness, ^{23}gentleness and self-control. Against such things there is no law. ^{24}Those who belong to Christ Jesus have crucified the flesh with its passions and desires. ^{25}Since we live by the Spirit, let us keep in step with **the Spirit**. ^{26}Let us not become conceited, provoking and envying each other.

I came to the conclusion the fruit of the spirit is the very nature of God and I wanted that in my life. I decided to apply mark 11:23 about believing what I say to the fruit of the spirit. I don't have these attributes I am love, I am joy, I am peace, I am forbearance, I am kindness, I am goodness, I am faithful, I am gentle, I am self-control. Speaking in this manner changed my thinking and attitudes towards others. When I was a delivery person for pizza shops I wanted a parting statement rather than have a good day which was cliché and everybody said it. So after talking to the Holy Spirit this simple phrase dropped in my heart, "enjoy your day." Then I had the thought do a word study on enjoy. I was pleased at the results, the en in front of joy meant to be empowered to have. So when I said enjoy your day I was empowering people to have joy which is the fruit of the spirit. I said this repeatedly for about a year and a half then I noticed a bank teller said that to me as I finished my business. It took that long but it came full circle proving to me that your words can affect others and yourself. My thinking and attitudes have changed where people have said to me they see Jesus in me. That is my agreement with John the Baptist He must increase and I must decrease.

    To many people use words to explain their circumstances and situations in life not realizing they will have more of what they say. They should be using words to change their lives and circumstances. I personally believe words are meant to change broken hearted, hard hearted and deceptive hearts into pure hearts before the Lord. What are you saying about yourself and others within the sphere of your influence?

28 DESIRE

What do you desire? When asked that question and answer quickly it will probably be flesh related. The more we speak life and blessing into our lives and the lives of others, we go from fleshly Christians to spiritual Christians.

Psalm 37:3-5 *Do Not Envy Those who Do Wrong*
...**3**Trust in the LORD and do good; dwell in the land and cultivate faithfulness. **4**Delight yourself in the LORD, and He will give you the desires of your heart. **5**Commit your way to the LORD; trust in Him, and He will do it. **6**He will bring forth your righteousness like the dawn, your justice like the noonday sun. **7**Be still before the LORD and wait patiently for Him; fret not

when men prosper in their ways, when they carry out wicked schemes. **8**Refrain from anger and abandon wrath; do not fret—it can only bring harm.

Philippians 3:9-10 *Knowing Christ Above All Else*

...**9**and be found in Him, not having my own righteousness from the law, but that which is through faith in Christ, the righteousness from God on the basis of faith. **10**I want to know Christ and the power of His resurrection and the fellowship of His sufferings, being conformed to Him in His death, **11**and so, somehow, to attain to the resurrection from the dead.

Romans 8:17

And if we are children, then we are heirs: heirs of God and co-heirs with Christ--if indeed we suffer with Him, so that we may also be glorified with Him

The more we fellowship with the Holy Spirit the more intimacy begins to develop. Soon an overwhelming love and fear will develop you. Fear not in being scared but an overwhelming respect and adoration that you don't want to say or do anything that will hurt him. As you continue your daily fellowship; not long winded elegant prayers that are religious sounding at best and filled with unbelief, but chatting about day's events. Talking about your job, shopping and even the weather you will grow in your relationship and have a greater understanding of how he thinks.

I will share two conversations I had with the Holy Spirit about the weather. The first time we had many days of rain and too much just wasn't a blessing. It finally stopped for a couple of hours but the forecast was for more rain coming in. I sat on my balcony and watched a thunder head moving in from the west so I asked God if He would get rid of it for us. I was surprised when I heard in my spirit "you do it." We were learning About authority in church so I thought I would give it a shot. I spoke to the thunder head and said I command you in the name of Jesus to go back west and drop your load over the ocean. I totally expected it to happen and wasn't surprised when the wind changed direction and the cloud moved west. I thanked God went inside and enjoyed nice sunny weather for a few weeks. The second time my cousin and I were doing a roofing Job and it became windy creating a difficult time to work. I prayed and asked God if He would stop the wind so we could finish the job. Instantly the wind stopped and became so calm you could blow smoke rings in the air and watch them for ten minutes. We finished the job and praised God for his help. The next day another job and the wind came up again so I asked God to stop it expecting the same thing. Pleasantly surprised I heard not today I am seeding the earth. I looked around and I could see pollen carrying seeds of plants flowers and other vegetation flying through the air. I mentioned it to my cousin and we praised God for a revelation of Him at work in the earth and nature. We finished the job just a bit later because of the wind.

Fellowship with the Holy Spirit will cause you to become more Christ like in nature for that is his assignment in the earth. I believe part of the Holy Spirit's work is to help you bring **Matthew 5:8** "Blessed are the pure in heart, for they shall see God, to fulfillment in your life. Not only see God the Father one day but see God at work in people's lives. Recognize their anointing's and gifts in their lives, honoring them and encouraging them to fulfill their destinies in

Christ.

My desire is to be more like Christ; hating sin but loving the sinner. To build strengthen and encourage His body to grow in relationship with Him and fulfill their destinies in Christ. If God showed us our destinies we would be flabbergasted because it's more than we can imagine or hope for.

Ephesians 2:7 in order that he may show in coming ages the super abounding riches of his grace in kindness toward us in Christ Jesus.

We are in the church age now. In eternity future how many and what kind of ages does God the Father have planned? Your heart condition matters, so go to the Holy Spirit and together work on creating a pure heart in you.

29 DESTINY AND PURPOSE

Is our destiny predetermined and the events that will happen to us are out of our control? Is there a hidden power controlling our future or do we have a choice in the matter?

Do I have to accept bad portions or can I change them? Do I want to control my own destiny with the limited understanding I have?

Shall I allow God's destiny for my life to be a model of liberty to the world?

By having a pure heart seeking after God we can ultimately find our purpose and destiny and be creatures of peace joy and contentment.

ABOUT THE AUTHOR
BIO

William carries the anointing of a prophet and psalmist. He is also a Bible teacher, author and international speaker. He operates in all of the Spiritual gifts. He uses the gifts as the Holy Spirit wills. One of William's great desires is to lead others to Christ and to follow Holy Spirit wherever He leads.

YOU CAN VISIT MY WEBSITE
WWW.PSALMISTWILLIAM.CA
FOR ENCOURAGING PSALMS AND TO BUY OTHER BOOKS I HAVE WRITTEN

www.ingramcontent.com/pod-product-compliance
Lightning Source LLC
Chambersburg PA
CBHW031426160426
43195CB00010BB/632